The Sporting Muse

The Sporting Muse

A Critical Study of Poetry about Athletes and Athletics

DON JOHNSON

McFarland & Company, Inc., Publishers
Jefferson, North Carolina, and London

LIBRARY OF CONGRESS CATALOGUING-IN-PUBLICATION DATA

Johnson, Don, 1942–
    The sporting muse : a critical study of poetry about athletes
and athletics / Don Johnson.
        p.   cm.
    Includes bibliographical references and index.

    ISBN 0-7864-1767-6 (softcover : 50# alkaline paper) ∞

    1. American poetry — History and criticism.   2. Athletics in
literature.   3. Athletes in literature.   4. Sports in literature.
I. Title.
PS310.A83J64   2004
811.009'357 — dc22   2004004056

British Library cataloguing data are available

Cover image: ©2004 Photodisc

Manufactured in the United States of America

McFarland & Company, Inc., Publishers
  Box 611, Jefferson, North Carolina 28640
    www.mcfarlandpub.com

For Jack Higgs, and in memory of Lyle Olsen–
competitors, inspirations

Table of Contents

Acknowledgments

Anonymous. "Cynisca," trans. Tom Dodge, is from *A Literature of Sports*. Quoted by permission of the translator.

Richard Behm. "The Origin and Purpose of Baseball" appeared in the *Quarterly West* 18 (Spring-Summer 1984). Quoted by permission of the author.

David Bottoms. "Sign for My Father, Who Stressed the Bunt" is from *Armored Hearts*, copyright © 1995 by David Bottoms. Quoted by permission of the author and Copper Canyon Press.

Neal Bowers. "Late Innings" appeared in *Helicon Nine* 19 (1988). Quoted by permission of the author. "Losing Season" appeared in *Arete* 3.2 (Spring 1986). Quoted by permission of the author.

Sharon Bryan. "In the Cheap Seats at the Kingdome" is from *Objects of Affection*, copyright © 1987 by Sharon Bryan. Quoted by permission of Wesleyan University Press.

Grace Butcher. "Runner Resumes Training After an Injury" appeared in *Before I Go Out on the Road*, copyright © 1979 by Grace Butcher. Quoted by permission of the author.

Bobby Byrd. "One of the Meanings of the 1987 NBA Championship Series" appeared in *Aethlon* 5.2 (Spring 1988). Quoted by permission of the author.

Doug Carlson. "Russ Joy Little League" appeared in *I Hate Long Goodbyes*, copyright © 1983 by Doug Carlson. Quoted by permission of the author.

Kent Cartwright. "Scoring" appeared in *Arete* 1.2 (Spring 1984). Quoted by permission of the author.

Acknowledgments

Fred Chappell. "Spitballer" and "Junk Ball" are from *The World Between the Eyes*, copyright © 1971 by Fred Chappell. Quoted by permission of Louisiana State University Press.

Tom Clark. "September in the Bleachers" is from *Blue*, copyright © 1974 by Tom Clark. Quoted by permission of the author.

Gregory Corso. "Dream of a Baseball Star" is from *Happy Birthday of Death*, copyright © 1960 by New Directions Publishing Corp. Quoted by permission of New Directions Publishing Corp.

Barbara Crooker. "Starving for the Gold" is from *In the Late Summer Garden*, copyright © 1998 by Barbara Crooker. Quoted by permission of the author.

Philip Dacey. "Mystery Baseball" is from *The Boy Under the Bed*, copyright © 1981 by Philip Dacey. Quoted by permission of the author.

Jim Daniels. "The Fat Man at the Ball Game" appeared in *Aethlon* 14.1 (Fall 1996). Quoted by permission of the author.

James Dickey. "For the Death of Lombardi" is from *The Central Motion: Poems, 1968–1979*, copyright © 1983 by James Dickey. "The Bee" is from *Poems 1957–1967*, copyright © 1967 by James Dickey. Both are quoted by permission of Wesleyan University Press.

Gregory Djanikian. "How I Learned English." Reprinted from *Falling Deeply into America* by permission of Carnegie Mellon University Press. Copyright © 1989 by Gregory Djanikian.

Jack Driscoll. "Touch Football" and "Boxing Towards My Birth" are from *Fishing the Backwash*, copyright © 1984 by Jack Driscoll. Quoted by permission of the author.

Stephen Dunn. "Day and Night Handball" from *New and Selected Poems 1974–1994* by Stephen Dunn. Copyright © 1994 by Stephen Dunn. Used by permission of W. W. Norton & Company, Inc.

David Allan Evans. "Bus Depot Reunion," "The Pole Vaulter," and "Watching Tackles in Slow Motion" are from *Train Windows*, copyright © 1976 by David Allan Evans. "Zen and the Art of Racquetball" appeared in *Aethlon* 12.1 (Fall 1994). Quoted by permission of the author.

Acknowledgments

Robert Francis. "The Base Stealer" is from *The Orb Weaver*, copyright © 1948 by Robert Francis. Quoted by permission of Wesleyan University Press.

Tess Gallagher. "Women's Tug of War at Lough Arrow" is from *Amplitude: New and Selected Poems*, copyright © 1978 by Tess Gallagher. Quoted by permission of Graywolf Press, Saint Paul, Minnesota.

Norman German. "New World in the Morning" appeared in *Worcester Review* 8.2 (Fall 1985). Quoted by permission of the author.

Charles Ghigna. "A Fighter Learns of Hands" appeared in *Arete* 2.2 (Spring 1985). Quoted by permission of the author.

Robert Gibb. "Listening to the Ballgame" is from *Momentary Days*, copyright © 1989 by Robert Gibb. "Night Basketball" appeared in *Arete* 3.2 (Spring 1986). Quoted by permission of the author.

Christopher Gilbert. "Charge" is from *Across the Mutual Landscape*, copyright © 1984 by Christopher Gilbert. Reprinted by permission of Graywolf Press, Saint Paul, Minnesota.

Gary Gildner. "Speaking in Tongues" and "In My Meanest Daydream" are from *The Warsaw Sparks*, copyright © 1990 by Gary Gildner. Reprinted by permission of the University of Iowa Press.

Judy Goldman. "Suicide" is from *Holding Back Winter*, copyright © 1987 by Judy Goldman. Quoted by permission of the author.

William Greenway. "Spider Drill" appeared in *Arete* 3.2 (Spring 1986). Quoted by permission of the author.

Robert Hamblin. "Half-Court Advantage" appeared in *Aethlon* 5.1 (Fall 1987). "Pick and Roll" appeared in *Aethlon* 8.2 (Spring 1991). Quoted by permission of the author.

William Heyen. "Mantle" and "The Stadium" are from *The Host: Selected Poems 1965–1990*, copyright © 1994 by William Heyen. Quoted by permission of Time Being Books.

Conrad Hilberry. "Stop Action" is from *Sorting the Smoke: New and Selected Poems*, copyright © 1990 by Conrad Hilberry. Quoted by permission of the University of Iowa Press. "Instruction" is from *Hummers,*

Acknowledgments

Knucklers and Slow Curves, copyright © 1990 by the University of Illinois Press. Quoted by permission of the author.

Edward Hirsch. "Execution" is from *The Night Parade*, copyright © 1989 by Edward Hirsch. Used by permission of Alfred A. Knopf, a division of Random House, Inc.

Jonathan Holden. "How to Play Night Baseball" and "Hitting Against Mike Cutler." Reprinted from *Design for a House: Poems*, by Jonathan Holden, by permission of the University of Missouri Press. Copyright © 1972 by Jonathan Holden. "Poem for Ed 'Whitey' Ford" reprinted from *Falling from Stardom* by permission of Carnegie Mellon University Press. Copyright © 1984 by Jonathan Holden.

Brooke Horvath. "Weathering March: Thoughts While Driving" is from *Arete* 2.2 (Spring 1985). Quoted by permission of the author.

Andrew Hudgins. Excerpt from "In the Red Seats" from *Babylon in a Jar: New Poems* by Andrew Hudgins, copyright © 1998 by Andrew Hudgins. Reprinted by permission of Houghton Mifflin Company. All rights reserved.

Richard Hugo. "From Altitude, the Diamonds." Copyright © 1980 by Richard Hugo, from *Making Certain It Goes On: Collected Poems of Richard Hugo*, by Richard Hugo. Used by permission of W. W. Norton & Company, Inc.

Richard Jackson. "Center Field" is from *Worlds Apart*, copyright © 1987 by Richard Jackson. Quoted by permission of the University of Alabama Press.

Rodney Jones. "The Sweep" is from *The Unborn*, copyright © 1985 by Rodney Jones. Quoted by permission of Grove/Atlantic, Inc.

Galway Kinnell. Excerpt from "On the Tennis Court at Night," from *Mortal Acts, Mortal Words* by Galway Kinnell. Copyright © 1980 by Galway Kinnell. Reprinted by permission of Houghton Mifflin Company. All rights reserved.

Phillip Levine. "The Right Cross" from *What Work Is* by Phillip Levine, copyright © 1991 by Philip Levine. Used by permission of Alfred A. Knopf, a division of Random House, Inc.

Acknowledgments

Lindner, Carl. "First Love" is from *Angling Into Light*, copyright © 2001 by Carl Lindner. Quoted by permission of the author. "When I Got It Right" is from *Shooting Baskets in a Dark Gymnasium*, copyright © 1984 by Carl Lindner. Quoted by permission of the author.

Michael McFee. "Shooting Baskets at Dusk" is from *Vanishing Acts*, copyright © 1989 by Michael McFee. Quoted by permission of Gnomon Press.

J. J. McKenna. Untitled poem is from *Arete* 4.1 (1986). Quoted by permission of the author.

William Matthews. Excerpt from "Caddies' Day, the Country Club, a Small Town in Ohio" from *Foreseeable Futures* by William Matthews. Copyright © 1992 by William Matthews. Excerpt from "Foul Shots, a Clinic," "A Happy Childhood," and "The Hummer" from *Selected Poems and Translations, 1969–1991* by William Matthews. Copyright © 1992 by William Matthews. Excerpt from "In the Cheap Seats at Cincinnati Gardens" from *Time and Money* by William Matthews. Copyright © 1995 by William Matthews. All are reprinted by permission of Houghton Mifflin Company. All rights reserved.

Peter Meinke. "To an Athlete Turned Poet" reprinted from *Trying to Surprise God*, by Peter Meinke, © 1981. Reprinted by permission of the University of Pittsburgh Press.

Justin Mitcham. "The Touch." Reprinted from *Somewhere in Ecclesiastes* by Justin Mitcham, by permission of the University of Missouri Press. Copyright © 1991 by Justin Mitcham.

Linda Mizejewski. "Season Wish" is from *Hummers, Knucklers, and Slow Curves*, copyright © 1990 by the University of Illinois Press. Quoted here by permission of the author.

Mariah Burton Nelson. "Competition" is from *Are We Winning Yet? How Women Are Changing Sports and Sports Are Changing Women*, copyright © 1991 by Mariah Burton Nelson. Used by permission of the author.

Tim Peeler. "Curt Flood" is from *Touching All the Bases*, copyright © 2000 by Tim Peeler. Used by permission of McFarland & Company.

Michael Rainnie. "Line Coach" is from *Aethlon* 8.1 (1990). Quoted by permission of the author.

Acknowledgments

Jack Ridl. "Good Training for Poetry" is from *Between,* copyright © 1988 by Jack Ridl. Quoted by permission of the author.

Timothy Seibles. "For Brothers Everywhere" is from *Hurdy Gurdy,* copyright © 1992 by Timothy Seibles. Quoted by permission of the author.

Anita Skeen. "Soccer by Moonlight" is from *More Golden Apples: A Further Celebration of Women and Sport,* Sandra Martz, ed., copyright © 1986 from Papier Mache Press. Quoted by permission of the author.

Danny Sklar. "Red Sox: 12 June, 1988." Used by permission of the author.

Arthur Smith. "Extra Innings" from *Elegy on Independence Day,* by Arthur Smith, copyright © 1985. Reprinted by permission of the University of Pittsburgh Press.

Dave Smith. "Blues for Benny Kid Paret" is from *Cumberland Station,* copyright © 1977 by Dave Smith. "Head Feint, Forearm, Glory" is from *The Fisherman's Whore,* copyright © 1974 by Dave Smith. "The Roundhouse Voices" is from *Goshawk, Antelope,* copyright © 1979 by Dave Smith. "Running Back" is from *In the House of the Judge,* copyright ©1983 by Dave Smith. All are quoted by permission of the author. "First Tournament, Learning Experience" is from *Fate's Kite,* copyright © 1995 by Dave Smith. Quoted by permission of Louisiana State University Press.

Ron Smith. "Noseguard" is from *Arete* 3.1 (1985). "Striking Out My Son in the Father-Son Game" is from *Running Again in the Hollywood Cemetery,* copyright © 1988 by Ron Smith. Used by permission of the author.

Alison Stone. "Nobody Left On" is from *Buffalo Spree* (Summer 1989). Quoted by permission of the author.

Mark Swanson. "Where It Begins" is from *Aethlon* 5.2 (Spring 1988). Quoted by permission of the author.

Rodney Torreson. "Ten Years Retired, Bobby Murcer Makes a Comeback Bid, 1985" is from *Aethlon* 4.1 (Fall 1986). Used by permission of the author.

John Updike. "Tao in the Yankee Stadium Bleachers" from *Collected Poems 1953–1993* by John Updike, copyright © 1993 by John Updike.

Acknowledgments

Acknowledgments

Used by permission of Alfred A. Knopf, a division of Random House, Inc.

Karen Volkman. "The Pregnant Lady Playing Tennis." Copyright © 1992 by Karen Volkman, from _Crash's Law_ by Karen Volkman. Used by permission of W. W. Norton & Company, Inc.

Wallace, Ronald. "The Friday Night Fights" from _The Uses of Adversity_, by Ronald Wallace, copyright © 1998. Reprinted by permission of the University of Pittsburgh Press.

Cary Waterman. "Last Game" is from _When I Looked Back You Were Gone_, copyright ©1992 by Cary Waterman. Quoted by permission of the author.

Don Welch. "To Bear Bryant, Somewhere on That Taller Tower" is from _Arete_ 2.1 (Fall 1984). Quoted by permission of the author.

Charles B. Wheeler. "Going to the Ballgame" is from _Aethlon_ 7.2 (Spring 1990). Quoted by permission of the author.

James Wright. "Autumn Begins in Martin's Ferry, Ohio," is from _Collected Poems_, copyright © 1971 by James Wright. Used by permission of Wesleyan University Press.

Preface

This study began with a strong perception on my part that poetry about sport has either been neglected or disregarded with a patronizing nod relegating it to the bottom level of a sub-genre. Equally strong was my sense that the volume of poems about sport was significant and that it was worthy of close analysis and praise. I think the case I have made in these pages more than supports those early assumptions.

Many people provided advice, information, and support with both the research and writing. I am especially grateful to East Tennessee State University's Office of Research and Sponsored Programs for a research grant which helped secure permissions. Dr. Judith Slagle, chair of the Department of English, provided support and a teaching schedule conducive to research and writing. Others, in no particular order of significance, include Bob Hamblin, Brooke Horvath, Jack Ridl, Jack Bedell, and Conrad Hilberry for help in locating poets; Jack Higgs, Tim Morris, Susan Bandy, Anne Darden, and Dave Smith for critical insight and encouragement; the inter-library loan staff of the Sherrod Library, especially Kelly Hensley, for securing innumerable volumes of poetry; Bert Bach for his friendship and tolerance; and Carolyn Novak for encouragement and understanding. Finally, heartfelt thanks go to Deanna Bryant for her help with formatting and organizing the manuscript.

Introduction

The earliest sport "literature" most certainly was poetry, whether in the form of tribal victory chants intoned around a campfire, or pre-homeric narratives of commemorative games and races declaimed at public forums. The recorded literature of antiquity is replete with celebratory odes, descriptive accounts of sporting contests, and satiric portraits of athletes in general, broad character types, and even specific individuals. Remarkably, the ancients anticipated almost every theme prevalent in contemporary American poetry about sports. Pindar bonded sport and religion in virtually all of his odes, and repeatedly suggested the potential for transcendence offered by athletic competition, what Richmond Lattimore describes in his translation of the odes as "a kind of transfiguration, briefly making radiant a world which most of the time seemed ... dark and brutal" (x). Both Homer and Virgil explored the nature of the contests they described in the *Iliad's* funeral games for Patroclus and those honoring Anchises in Book V of the *Aeneid*. Euripides in "Autolycus" warned his readers against attributing too much significance to athletes and their endeavors, and, by implication, condemned athletic "professionalism" as a waste of time and effort. Many of the ancients emphasized the violence inherent in sport, especially in wrestling, boxing, and the pankration, and the cumulative effects of that violence on the body, which, coupled with the toll nature exacts on us all, has always preoccupied the athlete with aging, and, ultimately, death. Like Homer's Nestor, every competitor must finally abandon the arena to younger athletes and "give way to the persuasions / of gloomy old age" (*Iliad*, Bk.23, *ll.*644–645, Lattimore trans., 467). Surprisingly, even what some might consider the exclusive province of contemporary literature, the role of women in sport, was anticipated by the anonymous Greek poet who wrote:

Introduction

I, Cynisca, who descend from Spartan kings,
Place this stone myself to mark
The race I won with my quick-footed steeds,
The only woman in all Greece to win.
[*A Literature of Sports*, Dodge trans., 344]

Each of these themes has found manifold expression in contemporary American poetry about sport. Nestor's complaint about growing old echoes in David Hilton's "I Try to Turn in My Jock," in Neil Weiss's "The Aging Athlete," and in Paul Petrie's "The Old Pro's Lament." The boxer in Lucilius's portrait who lost "a nose, a brow, eyelids, ears and chin" (*A Literature of Sports*, Dodge trans., 466), and thus sacrificed his patrimony when his own father failed to recognize him, is mirrored by Alan Dugan's Hurricane Jackson, who at the end of his career has become virtually unrecognizable after years of being mutilated in the ring.

Parallels between ancient and contemporary sports poems are readily available, but there are significant differences as well. American sports poems have always tended to be essentially democratic, their "heroes" not paragons of strength and virtue, but only slightly larger versions of ourselves. It's worth noting, in fact, that our most famous "hero" in a sports poem, Thayer's Casey, is a failure. Classical athletic contests were exclusive, their competitors exemplars. Ours tend to be inclusive and participatory. Baseball's popularity among the masses as a vehicle for the demonstration of their common exuberance made the sport appealing to Walt Whitman. He reveled in the common folks' "enjoying picnics or jigs or a good game of base-ball" ("Song of Myself" sect. 33, 122). And while Whitman's descendants in American poetry have celebrated their share of Ruths, Mantles, and Lombardis, their focus, when not on the essence of a particular sport, is more likely to have been on the ordinary athlete (in this case a golfer) that Cary Waterman eulogizes in "Last Game," or the high school football coach of Edward Hirsch's "Execution." Of the 108 poems collected in *This Sporting Life: Contemporary American Poems About Sports and Games* (1987), for example, only seven can be even broadly interpreted as dealing with famous athletes, and this number includes a poem about the Greek runner Kalamachius and one about Ulysses. Granted, this anthology, edited by Emilie Buchwald and Ruth Roston, treats sport with a great deal of latitude, including poems about snorkeling, juggling and marbles playing, but this breadth simply reinforces the argument for democratization. In *Line Drives: 100 Contemporary Baseball Poems* (2002), the only poem focused exclusively on a major league ballplayer is Gary Fincke's "The Career of Lou Proctor," about a non-existent player erroneously assigned to the St. Louis Browns. A telegraph operator added Proctor's name to one box score and he was listed in six editions of *The Baseball Digest* until the error was discovered and the name dropped.

Our sports poems have also become, especially in the last thirty years, increasingly domestic, with games and contests, and their attendant anxieties, complexities, as well as opportunities for the demonstration of *arête* (striving for excellence), providing a matrix for family relationships. Surprisingly, familial relations are a common theme even in poems about boxing. Michael Oriard, in an article entitled "From Jane Allen to *Water Dancer*: A Brief History of the Feminist (?) Sports Novel," argues that the increased attention to family values was one of the earliest contributions women made to sports *fiction*. Sharon Carson and Brooke Horvath, citing such examples as Betty Adcock's "The Sixth Day," Nancy Jones's "Running Blind," and Mabel M. Kuykendall's "Baseball Pitcher," see a similar pattern in sports poetry by women ("Women's ... Poetry"). The case for poetry is more difficult to support, however, simply because there are so many examples, and arguments of influence are impossible to substantiate. Philip Booth's "First Lesson" (*A Literature of Sports*, 336), a poem about a father teaching his young daughter to swim, predates any of the examples cited by Carson and Horvath by a decade. James Wright's "Autumn Begins in Martin's Ferry, Ohio," a poem about high school football players sacrificing themselves in an attempt to insure their parents' sexual vitality, was published in 1963, well before most of the poems Carson and Horvath mention. The question of direct influence aside, the fact remains that our sports poems no longer limit family issues to considerations of patrimony as did the ancients. And if the women were not the first, theirs are certainly the most insistent voices arguing for sports' blending with domestic issues, and vice versa. No longer is it "always ... fathers and sons," as Roger Kahn would have it (5). It is fathers and daughters and mothers and sons, aunts and uncles, husbands and wives.

Introduction

It follows almost naturally, then, given their personal nature, that the dominant tone of our sports poems would be nostalgic, the favored point of view, first person. Since Wordsworth, with the exception of the work of the high modernists, most of our poetry has been about ourselves, either as a record of experience or a vehicle for the creation of a personal mythology. Often the two aims coalesce, as in Wordsworth's *The Prelude*. Most American sports poems oscillate between these two functions with memory as catalyst. There are notable exceptions to this tendency, of course. One thinks of Robert Francis's pitcher who throws in an eternal present, or his two uncoached boys forever "tossing a poem together" in "Catch" (*Collected Poems*). But most of our sports poems are recalled from memory, even if their speakers are not so much participants in a sport as what Christian Messenger refers to in *Sport and the Spirit of Play in Contemporary American Fiction* as *witnesses* to an event which elevated or involved them in a critical capacity (210–47).[1] Donald Hall speculates that one of the reasons baseball in particular appeals so to poets is that it takes us back to our childhoods, but the operative word here is as much *back* as it is *childhood* (62). Football poems take us back to adolescence, basketball to early adulthood. As M. L. Rosenthal points out in *Poetry and the Common Life*, the "passion — to remember and retain what inevitably we must lose — is the first powerful sound of art" (19). Rosenthal goes on to capture the essence of both poetry and the sporting experience, and in the process explains most poets' attraction for sports, when he asserts that

> memory is the key to communion, bringing people into sympathy, and art of every kind adds to the range of communion by revealing precise shadings of the experience to others. In a very broad sense, poetry can be seen as a way of making available to our memories, through language, the private relation each person has to the world [27].

Obviously, all sports poems are not intimate accounts of experiences. Many feature larger-than-life athletes, but their roles are, more often than not, decidedly unheroic. With some notable exceptions (Donald Peterson's "Ballad of the Dead Yankees," Samuel Allen's "Satch," and Tom Clark's elegies for Roberto Clemente, as examples), these poems reveal great athletes as susceptible to the same fears and temptations as the rest of us. In "Mantle," William Heyen describes the Yankee slugger's selling out by advertising Brylcreem in television commercials, and plants the seeds of his corruption in his childhood training by a demanding father. Randall Jarrell, in "Say Goodbye to Big Daddy," laments the death (as a result of a heroin overdose) of the former Baltimore Colts tackle, and records his having said that he was scared most of his life, though "You wouldn't think so to look at me. / It gets so bad I cry myself to sleep" (*Complete Poems*, 344). In "Dream of a Baseball Star" Gregory Corso envisions a mythic Ted Williams at the plate while God burns in fiery fast balls. Despite the poet's desperate plea for a home run, Williams, like Casey, strikes out.

Many factors have influenced the athletes' loss of heroic stature in our culture: the media's close scrutiny of their lives; the huge sums of money which corrupt amateurs and transform professionals into celebrities and corporations; and also a pervasive cynicism, to which the aforementioned factors contribute, which casts suspicion on what appears to be heroic behavior in any arena of public life. Paradoxically, while the potential for heroism in sports has all but disappeared, the impact of sport on our lives has never been greater.

The influence of sport on American culture has grown exponentially in the last quarter century. The number of people engaged in sports and games has never been greater, and the age at which they begin participating seems to become lower with each passing year. On the other hand, the longevity of older athletes is constantly being extended. In addition, the number of available sporting activities, especially those "opened up" to women, has increased dramatically. Jogging, racquetball, tee-ball, soccer, roller-blade hockey, and "extreme sports" involve not only athletes "stolen" from other sports, but countless players who, if not for these modes of recreation, would not have been participants at all. Golf and tennis have become essentially middle-class sports, popular enough to generate commercial revenue on both network and cable television, which now features an all-golf channel. It is difficult to assess the impact the sheer volume of television sports coverage has on our lives. Sporting events can be tuned in around the clock, and when the events themselves are not being aired, the viewer is subjected to analyses of games, or commercials in which athletes promote such widely diverse products as underwear and kielbasa.

Introduction

Sport touches us all. Its influence extends beyond Jacques Barzun's assertion that in order to understand America we must first understand baseball. While there may be something intrinsically "American" about baseball, sports in general are so pervasive in our lives that efforts to understand and come to terms with those lives must, almost of necessity, include sports, a fact which helps to explain the proliferation of sports books—team histories, biographies, exposés, novels and short stories—on the market since the early sixties. As an example of the current popularity of sports books, each spring the *New York Times Book Review* features reviews of books on baseball alone which fill over half of this opening-week-of-the-season special issue. And poets have kept pace with writers in other fields, proportionally, though not in terms of sheer volume.[2]

The degree to which sports are important to contemporary American poets is underscored by the following comment Dave Smith made to an interviewer from *Graham House Review* (Spring 1982):

> Bill Heyen wrote me once that it was odd how all the best poets are ex-jocks. If you allow his term to include people who recognize and delight in grace of the body, then you want to say yes. Frost, baseball; Kumin, swimming; Jarrell, tennis; Ransom, baseball; Whitman, baseball; Keats, [Byron?] swimming. It goes on. And speaking of Ransom, he has a wonderful line: what a poet must have in the right order is the head, the heart, and the foot. That's a physical description of a rhythmic and intellectual activity, of poetry [67].

Smith's explicit connection of poetry and sports as "rhythmic and intellectual" activities, combined with M. L. Rosenthal's notion of poetry as "communion," also explains the appeal of sports as the subject of self-reflexive poetry, poems which are ultimately about the writing of poetry. Baseball more than any other sport has lent itself to this kind of writing. One thinks of Mike Shannon's "The Art of Baseball Poetry," of Robert Francis's "Pitcher," and of Jack Ridl's "Good Training for Poetry." But Peter Meinke's "To an Athlete Turned Poet" in which he describes James Dickey as exchanging the defensive lines on the football field for lines in poetry, and transferring the rage and exuberance of the game to "words words words" (*Trying*, 69), is a fine example as well. Meinke, in

24

fact, intuited Dickey's intention to create what he felt was a "new kind of poetry." He wanted to infuse his work with a "fast, athletic, imaginative, and muscular vigor" (*Summer*, 15) that he found lacking in the poetry available to him in the early fifties. A strong case for reflexivity could also be made for David Allan Evans's "Pole Vaulter," who leaps

> never forcing myself
> trusting it is right
> to be taken to the end
> of tension poised
> for the powerful thrust to
> fly me beyond expectation
> [*Train Windows*, 3]

as an appropriate description of any poet's goal.

Other prominent contemporary poets who have written on sports or their own sporting experiences include Richard Hugo, Robert Penn Warren, William Carlos Williams, John Updike, and Dave Smith himself, as well as Tess Gallagher, May Swenson, and Babette Deutsch. Interestingly enough, George Plimpton in *The Norton Book of Sports* not only ignores for the most part the significant contribution of poems to the literature of sport, and to contemporary literature in general, he actually enlists the aid of two poets to minimize that significance. Plimpton writes:

> It has always puzzled me why poets have not devoted more of their skills to sports subjects; so many of the ingredients seem involved — triumph, despair, prowess, beauty, the oft-quoted idea that sport is a microcosm of life itself. Yet an anthology of great poetry, a thousand pages long, will include A. E. Houseman's [sic] "To An Athlete Dying Young," and little else [16].

Obviously, the operative phrase in Plimpton's comment is "great poetry." Most anthologies of contemporary American poetry contain many examples of sports poems, and even if Plimpton could argue that these poems are not "great" literature, how could he ignore the significant body of sporting poetry passed down to us from the ancients? The poetry on field sports in Pope's "Windsor Forest," or Gay's "Rural Sports"? Wordsworth's skating scene from *The Prelude?*

Plimpton cites Donald Hall's agreement with him that though "hundreds of poems have been written about sports almost invariably all are second rate" (16). He then quotes Hall's assertions that "poems should never be *about* anything" (16), and that he [Hall] doesn't "take sport seriously. That's what so wonderful about it" (17). The time he has dedicated to sporting endeavors (Plimpton cites Hall's "participatory stint" with the Pittsburgh Pirates), and the care and effort that went into *Fathers Playing Catch with Sons*, give the lie to Hall's last comment. If Hall intends by his remark about the seriousness of sport something close to what he has articulated in "Baseball and the Meaning of Life," that "baseball sets off the meaning of life precisely because it is pure of meaning," Plimpton must take his quote from Hall too lightly, since the poet goes on to argue in his essay that,

> as the ripples in the sand (in the Kyoto garden) organize and formalize the dust which is dust, so the diamonds and rituals of baseball create an elegant, trivial, enchanted grid on which our suffering, shapeless sinful day leans for the momentary grace of order [*Fathers*, 51].

Essentially, Hall is arguing here that the game is autotelic, one of those activities that have, in the words of A. Bartlett Giamatti, "no purpose except fully to be themselves" (15). The less important the sporting event in the real world, the more important it becomes as sport. Hall's comment that poetry should not be *about* anything is consistent with the tone of Plimpton's argument, but too precious to refute. William Matthews makes a similar point about poetry, which Horvath and Wiles cite as a rationale for poetry about sport, saying that "to speak in terms of subject matter is somehow never to speak adequately of poetry, which chooses its provisional subject 'in order to be transformed' (143) that it provide the occasion for passionate attention and articulate reflection" (*Line Drives*, xxi).[3] And as for the notion that most sports poems are second-rate, Hall knows full well that *most* poems written by anyone, at any time, on any subject are second-rate, or worse.

Plimpton's other poet, Robert Bly, argues that the ancients wrote interesting poetry about sport, but with the advent of Christianity "the poets' attention shifted to losers, love unrequited, victims of society, the struggles of the meek, 'people who get beaten up a lot'" (*Norton*, 17). Bly also argues that sport is considered too trivial for serious literary consideration, a point which, from one perspective, at least, flies directly in the face of Hall's comment that baseball is "pure of meaning." Both arguments would apply with equal strength to fiction and the essay, and the first applies to virtually any literature written after the fall of the Roman Empire. I should point out, too, that Plimpton includes poems by both Bly and Hall in the anthology.

Like Plimpton, critics have also tended to underrate or ignore the substantial body of contemporary sporting poems, authored by an impressive list of poets, and have focused instead almost exclusively on sport fiction, or even non-fiction prose such as that collected each year in *The Best Sports Writing* anthology. The criticism of sports poetry, as sports poetry, has been limited to David Allen Evans's distinction between participatory and non-participatory types in "Poetry and Sport," and Sharon Carson's and Brooke Horvath's "Women's Sports Poetry: Some Observations and Representative Texts." In addition, two studies offer analyses of the sports poems of specific poets: Philip Dacey's "Challenging Chronos: The Sports Poetry of David Allan Evans," and Carson's and Horvath's "Running in Place: The Lines and Miles of Grace Butcher's Life and Work." Finally, David Vanderwerken's analysis of James Dickey's "For the Death of Lombardi" provides a detailed reading of that poem along with relevant commentary on sports, coaching and the manifold interpretations of success.

The critics' neglect (and Plimpton's dismissal) of sport poetry can be attributed to neither a dearth of material nor the quality of available work. Rather it derives from the almost paradoxical combination of a given poet's expression of an exclusive vision in a vibrant and unique language with the mundane and readily apprehended language of sport. The problem is summed up in Terrence J. Roberts's presidential address to the 1994 meeting of the Philosophic Society for the Study of Sport. Poets with sport as their subject risk not being taken seriously because they are "speaking of society's playtime with language's dreamtime" (*Journal of the Philosophy of Sport*, 95). Relying on the work of Harold Bloom and Richard Rorty, Roberts laments the "impoverished language that determines conventional descriptions of elite sport" (98). He blames the "blindly cruel and humiliating language" used to "redescribe" athletes for the "loss of self" they suffer as a result of their success on the field or court (98). He then challenges athletes to redefine themselves in Bloomian terms, to become "strong poets" with sport as their medium of expression. Roberts concedes that the "redescription of sport as poetry and of the strong athlete as the strong maker is sketchy, tentative, and highly speculative" (105), but in making his case he illuminates the obstacles genuine poets of sport must overcome, and the difficult path he or she must travel to achieve legitimacy.

If one were to look for a model of success in writing poems about sporting experience, he might do no better than to cite the most recent work of Nobel Laureate Seamus Heaney, arguably the most influential voice in contemporary poetry in English. In Heaney's last three volumes, *Seeing Things* (1991), *The Spirit Level* (1996), and *Electric Light* (2001), sport and play have become dominant motifs. In *Seeing Things* such poems as "Markings" (about children laying out an impromptu pitch and playing football), and the third poem in his "Squarings" sequence (about a game of marbles), argue for a kind of muscular equanimity as the basis for childhood vision. Child's play is for Heaney in *Seeing Things* a vehicle through which vision can be attained and recaptured, not merely through the memory of exceeding the limits of the phenomenal world through sport and play, but through actually reenvisioning those memories through a mature perspective, through eyes that, according to Helen Vendler, have become "intensely perceptive by unignorable annihilation" (*Seamus Heaney* 138). Play is also a source of imaginative energy in *The Spirit Level*, but in the later volume Heaney evokes memories of play in an effort to restore equilibrium, not so much to transcend reality but to endure it.

Heaney's reenvisioning comes remarkably close to Roberts's *re-redescription*, the doubled prefix indicating that

> the language that currently occupies our strongholds of conventional sporting truths, thereby affecting most literal descriptions (and perhaps depictions) of sport is dominant not because of some neat and demonstrated correspondence with reality, but as a result of previous, powerful, but

nonetheless contingent metaphorical redescriptions that shattered some longstanding but increasingly feeble literal truths [98].

A clue to Heaney's method appears in a critical comment he makes in *The Redress of Poetry* (1995) about Robert Frost's description of the children's playhouse in "Directive" as an example of the poet's "imaginative transformation of human life ... the means by which we can most truly grasp it and comprehend it" (xv). The children's playthings, old dishes and utensils from the real house, fed their fantasies, which became "a kind of freely invented answer to everything experienced in the 'house in earnest' where (the tone makes this clear) life was lived in sorrow and anger" (xv). Heaney urges us to take seriously Frost's approach to child's play in "Directive," and he follows Frost's model triumphantly in his recent work, celebrating pick-up football games, marbles, word games, make-believe journeys and the exhilaration of swinging amidst the "give and take of branches" (a direct nod to Frost?).

With his reliance on games and play and the physical objects associated with them, Heaney illustrates in his later work the evolution of what he has termed "instinctual ballast," what might be thought of as the poet's imaginative lodestone, a firm grounding securing an identity productive of insight and vision. Heaney's celebration of childhood games is a direct response to Rorty's observation that

> the best way to cause people long-lasting pain is to humiliate them by making the things that seemed most important to them look futile, obsolete and powerless. Consider what happens when a child's precious possessions— the little things around which he weaves his fantasies that make him a little different from other children — are described as "trash," and thrown away [*Contingency*, 89–90].

Like Frost, Heaney illustrates in his poems of play and games, "the imagination pressing back against reality," both as a response to pain and injustice, and as a countervailing power. It is instructive to note that he describes poetry as "a matter of angelic potential, a *motion* [italics mine] of the soul" (*Redress*, 192).[4]

Introduction

When sports poems are successful, they do generate a "motion of the soul." They do allow the "imagination to press back against reality" and build the instinctual ballast necessary for the poet's confidence in his or her own voice. The following pages represent my attempt to draw attention to such contemporary sports poems and place them in a cultural and literary perspective. Rather than singling out individual poets for lengthy analyses, I have focused chapters on poems about the three major sports in the United States: baseball, football, and basketball, not so much in an effort to exhaust the possibilities offered by a particular game as to determine whether or not there are broad, common attitudes and values which both reflect and color our views of a given sport. I have avoided comment on field sports such as fishing and hunting as well as extended theoretical arguments regarding fine distinctions among play, games, and sports. Moreover, I have chosen not to emphasize critical theory, preferring to focus on primary material, since much of it is relatively unknown, and nothing has been written about it as a body of material. The chapter on women's poetry is an exception, however, since so much of what has been said of women's writing in general is inextricably bound up in feminist theory.

The chapter on baseball is, of necessity, the most comprehensive, for two reasons: more and better poems have been written about baseball than any other sport; and assumptions and approaches are established in this chapter which the entire volume tests and explores, although the second chapter, on poems about football, is nearly as long for the same reasons. Chapter III looks at basketball poems, and the fourth examines sports poems by and about women. Obviously there will be some overlap here, since women write poems about baseball, tennis, and other sports, and some of their poems are about men engaged in sport. On the other hand, many men have written about women's involvement in sports either as participants or spectators. At any rate, the amount of poetry by and about women more than justifies the shift in my perspective. My fifth chapter looks at less dominant sports: golf, racquet sports and boxing, sports chosen both because of the number of poems written about them, and because these poems demonstrate that poets define as well as reflect our attitudes toward particular sports. Since it would have been nearly impossible to comment on all "minor" sports, I have used these as representative examples. Chapter VI focuses on the sports spectator in poetry, onlookers who range in their degree of involvement in the game from the rabid fan in David Allen Evans's "Will You Sign My Brand New Baseball, Louie?" to the irritated apartment dweller in Alison Stone's "Nobody Left On" who overhears her neighbor's enthusiastic response to a Mets/Dodgers game on the radio and mistakes it for the sounds of good sex.

My conclusion argues that sports poetry as a whole constitutes a body of material substantial enough not only to justify this study, but to generate others as well, though I have concentrated on the best and most representative poems about particular sports rather than attempting merely to enumerate as many examples as possible.

I

"Who the Hell Are You, Kid?"

Language, Nostalgia and Identity in the Baseball Poem[1]

Imitating Archibald MacLeish's "Ars Poetica," Mike Shannon summarizes his argument for naturalness and originality in poems about baseball by simply asserting that a baseball poem should be "Poetry" (*Aethlon* 4.2, 146). Following as it does on the heels of such baseball terminology as "high and tight," and "caught in the pocket," Shannon's seemingly reductive assertion echoes the paradox of MacLeish's didactic argument for non-didactic poetry — "A poem should not mean / But be" (*Collected Poems*, 41). Moreover, Shannon's assertion suggests the equation between the game and poetry that W. P. Kinsella states categorically — "Baseball is poetry" (*Hummers*, xvii) — and underscores the richness, variety and inclusiveness that characterize the contemporary American baseball poem.

Kinsella explains that the very nature of baseball makes it "conducive to poetry and fiction." It is a game of silences and anticipation, an open-ended endeavor without limits of time or space (*Hummers*, xviii). Other arguments for the link between baseball and writing abound. Cordelia Candelaria's list of nine characteristics of the game is the most exhaustive. She cites baseball's genesis in "aboriginal myth," its development through the "active, changing lives of numerous folk societies," its fulfillment of basic restorative human needs as physical play, relaxation, and fun and its role in satisfying our "agonistic" appetites. She further notes baseball's links with our national history and political life, its fictive source in the Doubleday myth, and the wealth of symbols the game offers (13–14). In "The Origin and Purpose of Baseball" Richard Behm fixes the game's origins on a mythical veldt where a mother pulls down the moon thinking it is an egg her children can eat. The mother and the moon impose an order on the chaos of childhood:

> rules based on the rhythms
> of the sea, birth, the geometry
> of hope, the mysteries
> of nines and threes
> ...
>
> [*Quarterly West* 18, 98]

Denis Porter reinforces Kinsella's comments about the rich possibilities of baseball's spatial metaphors, and articulates its oft-acknowledged potential for myth — setting out from "home" on a quest, encountering the perils of the journey and, with skill, luck, and the aid of companions, returning "home" (147–51).[3]

Donald Hall argues that baseball is "the poet's game." He cites John Crowe Ransom's claim for baseball's affinity with the pastoral, allowing for a "world that is small, exact, formal, whole, pleasing, and separate from ordinary reality: a green island in a sea of change." The best baseball poems, Hall says, "pay attention to small things" — the turn of a batter's head, a base stealer's almost imperceptible list toward the base he covets, a pitcher's scowl — all "acts of attention seen through the microscope of the pastoral." Then again, Hall almost casually comments that baseball might be the game of poets for the simple reason that "all of us need regularly to revisit childhood" (*Fathers*, 62).

Hall's explanation, emphasizing attention to detail, the creation of "green islands" and a return to childhood, could also be a prescription for poetry in general, especially poetry written since 1798, thus reinforcing Kinsella's equation of the game and poetry, and perhaps accounting for the self-reflexive nature of so many baseball poems. It also renders doubly ironic Hall's more recent comments to George Plimpton regarding the relative inconsequence of sports poetry in general.

Two other factors have enhanced baseball's popularity with poets in particular. First, the prolific outpouring and cumulative influence of successful baseball literature have legitimized the use of the game as subject, and for the American male poet, in fact, have made it almost obligatory. The second factor is the game's ubiquity and adaptability. Baseball means the American and National Leagues, pennant races culminating in contemporary America's version of primitive cultures' autumn harvest festival, the World Series. But baseball is also long bus rides in Class C and D leagues, dusty afternoons in near-empty ballparks in towns such as Elizabethton, Tennessee, or Helena, Montana. Baseball is college ball, high school, American Legion, Babe Ruth and Little League, pickup games in sandlots and pastures, family games of catch in backyards, softball, stickball, tennis-ball-against-the-wall ball. Thus many baseball poems define the game by illuminating our transformations of a contest meant to be played by eighteen players on a large field into a competition between four kids to a side on a city street, or two imagined teams battling it out in the head of a single youngster throwing a wet tennis ball at a garage door.

Given baseball's rich history, and baseball poetry's origins (at least in the popular imagination) in the heroic realm, it would be logical to assume that poems about baseball would celebrate the game's heroes and reflect its role in the evolution of the American experience. Candelaria argues that "Casey at the Bat" "encapsulates three important themes: the fall of a folk hero, its effect on his community, and the meaning of both to the universe of humans" (22–23). But although the "interactive resonance between ballplayer-hero, fans, diamond, and beyond vibrates powerfully in the baseball *fiction* [italics mine] that followed" Thayer's poem, baseball *poetry*, especially that published after 1960, tends to function on a more private level.

Obviously, there are exceptions to this tendency, poetic tributes to bygone times and their heroes such as Donald Petersen's "The Ballad of Dead Yankees," an unabashed paean to Babe Ruth and his teammates reminiscent of Grantland Rice's eulogy for the Sultan of Swat. Other poems contain tributes of varying length and intensity to such notables as Ted Williams, Carl Yastrzemski, Bobby Murcer, Luis Aparicio, Lou Brock, Bob Gibson, and Roberto Clemente. Samuel Allen in "To Satch (Or American Gothic)" records the legendary pitcher's dream of immortality, of someday grabbing a "handfulla stars" and whipping three sizzling strikes down from heaven. He would then look over at the Almighty in anticipation of His approval (*motion*, 20).

Employing virtually identical imagery, although in a more surrealistic setting, Gregory Corso in "Dream of a Baseball Star" records a more pessimistic, and altogether more common, contemporary attitude toward the game's heroes as epitomized by Ted Williams. Corso dreams of Williams leaning against the Eiffel Tower, which he apparently equals in height. The "Splendid Splinter" flings

> his schoolboy wrath
> toward some invisible pitcher's mound
> —waiting the pitch all the way from heaven.

The pitches come by the hundreds, "all afire," but Williams goes down swinging and Corso's speaker cries out in his dream:

> God! throw thy merciful pitch!
> Herald the crack of bats!
> Hooray the sharp liner to left!
> Yea the double, the triple!
> Hosannah the home run!
> [*Happy Birthday*, 45]

Obviously, more is going on here than just a mythical face off between batter and pitcher. When Williams, the perennial bad boy (Corso, echoing Randall Jarrell, also calls him a poet), openly taunts the Ultimate Fireballer but fails to connect, the dreamer asks for mercy, not merely for Williams, but for the rest of us as well. Candelaria's assessment of Casey's failure applies equally well to Williams's cosmic K: the batter's Bunyanesque stature clearly qualifies him as a folk hero; his fall affects the community (represented by the speaker's desperate pleas), and resonates in the "universe of humans" at large as the cosmic nature of the face-off emphasizes.

Tim Peeler applauds Curt Flood, in a poem which bears his name, for sacrificing his career for those who came after him, but the poet's assertion that

> you [Flood] are a ghost at barterer's wing,
> your smokey gray eyes

> are two extra zeroes
> on every contract
>
> [*Touching,* 17]

praises Flood's selflessness while reducing his legacy to purely monetary terms.

In "Mantle" William Heyen records his disappointment at the great Yankee slugger's failure to retire before his diminishing talents tarnished his image. Mantle then sold himself in Brylcreem commercials where "models with open mouths draped around him / as they never were in Commerce, Oklahoma" where he grew up. Heyen takes the reader back to Mantle's boyhood, back to the workouts with his father who trained the young prospect to switch hit:

> his father winged them in,
> and the future blew toward him
>
> now a fastball, now a slow
> curve hanging
> like a model's smile.
>
> [*The Host,* 72]

suggesting that the seeds for Mantle's corruption were planted early on in the fertile soil of that Oklahoma barnyard.

While Williams fails to perform heroically, Flood's heroism is confined to the negotiating table. Mantle's heroism is tarnished by early training which encouraged his commodification, the Brylcreem commercials simply reinforcing his own image as product. With their focus on recognized baseball stars and especially with Heyen's emphasis on Mantle's selling out, "Dream of a Baseball Star," "Curt Flood," and "Mantle" conform more closely to the view of baseball offered by most prose writers both in fiction and non-fiction. Baseball poems, on the other hand, tend not to deal with history as history, commercialization, sociology, or strategy. In a review essay on Jerry Klinkowitz's *Writing Baseball* and *Hummers, Knucklers and Slow Curves,* Warren Goldstein argues that

> poems ... are not going to be much help if you want to know
> how baseball came to be, where it was born in American

culture, how it grew, where players came from, how money has changed the game, how and why the color line was drawn and breached, or when the stolen base makes sense ["Inside Baseball," 422].

Neither do baseball poets tend to indulge in rhapsodic tributes to the game's giants in the mode of Roger Angell, Roger Kahn, or W. P. Kinsella. Poets tend to take a darker look and to focus on more local conditions. They allow us, in Goldstein's words,

> to understand how the game lives in the minds of fans, why grown men and women cling to it so tenaciously — despite George Steinbrenner and "the wave" and twenty-nine-million-dollar contracts and drug testing and Walter O'Malley's treachery and Ty Cobb's racism and "King" Kelly's boozing and Al Spaulding's opportunism... [422].

Baseball lives in the words of its poets first as a game closely scrutinized and celebrated for its finesse, its balance and symmetry, its potential as a source of aesthetic pleasure, vital language and mystery. Poets such as Robert Fitzgerald, Robert Francis, Fred Chappell, and Robert Wallace have watched the game closely. They understand it. Their poems allow a reader insight into baseball which even years of untutored observation might not reveal. Other poets (perhaps the majority), while appreciating the game as game, look to baseball as primarily a source of memories, a vehicle for identity.

In "Cobb Would Have Caught It" Robert Fitzgerald records the cumulative activities that make up a Sunday afternoon ball game in Anywhere, U.S.A.: the baseman charging in to scoop up a grounder and winging it to first; the catcher squatting in the dust; the pitcher, who rubs the ball before delivering it to the batter who digs in at the plate and then sends a long fly ball to the outfielder who chases it, but fails to make the catch [thus the title]. Fitzgerald spices his narrative with what passes for baseball lingo — "Oh attaboy, attyoldboy," "wings it deadeye," and "socko, baby" (*Spring Shade*, 66) — and he faithfully records the sequence of activities that make up a "play" in baseball. He manages even to reproduce the spirit of a hot afternoon of sandlot baseball. He fails, however, to capture the muscular tension, the quickness of movement, balance and recovery inherent in the dance which is baseball.

No one has captured the balletic potential in baseball better than Robert Francis. His catalogue of small details entitled "The Base Stealer" fully realizes the physical and mental tension, the interaction between runner and pitcher, and the split-second timing which base stealing demands. His poised runner bounces on "tiptoe like a dropped ball / Or a kid skipping rope." He "teeters, skitters, tingles, and teases," taunting the opposition, trying to draw a throw to the base, to disrupt the pitcher's rhythm, or to sense the exact second he decides to go to the plate. He hangs there, "Delicate, delicate, delicate, delicate," waiting for the poet's final explosive word signaling his almost imperceptible weight shift, his absolute commitment — "now!" (*The Orb Weaver*, 7).

Similarly, Robert Wallace's "The Double Play" displays one of poetry's advantages over prose as a vehicle for describing sporting events — its immediacy, the ability to collapse time into a moment in which successive steps in a process are perceived as occurring almost simultaneously. Wallace suggests that while the pitcher's arm is in motion the double play begins to develop. As the ball is hit, the shortstop both "scoops to his right" and whirls, "redirects its flight" to the second baseman who is "running poised." He then "pirouettes" to throw to the "leaning- / out first baseman" who "ends the dance." The play is "too swift for deception / is final, lost, among the loosened figures" who jog off the field. The entire play, Wallace records, takes place "in the space where the poem has happened" (*Views from a Ferris Wheel*, 27). It is no accident, either, that Wallace packs his kinetic verbs and rich participles into one sentence.

Ironically, Conrad Hilberry captures the flow of baseball in a piece called "Stop Action." Comparing the shortstop's snatching up a grounder to "an underwater dance," Hilberry freezes the action as the ball leaves the infielder's hand, noting that the play generates in its viewers "a curious poignancy, / a catch in the throat," that occurs in any worthwhile moment caught between the initiation and the completion, what Hilberry calls "the absolute moment," which

> gathers the surge
> and muscle of the past, complete
> yet hurling itself forward —
> [*Sorting*, 67]

In detailing these plays unique to baseball, Francis, Wallace and Hilberry adopt an approach which, more than any other technique, aligns them with poets who describe other sports. Francis has himself, in fact, closely observed other sports for relatively impersonal (third person), yet wholly sympathetic (in every sense of the term) accounts of their participants in action as in "Skier," "The Swimmer," and "Two Wrestlers." Other poems which apply Francis's approach to different sports are Don Welch's "High Jumper" and Kent Cartwright's "Scoring" (basketball), both of which feature "attention to small things" (Hall, 62), and a suspension of physical laws. Players hang in the air, and time either slows down or envelops what should be sequential activities in one nearly-synchronous movement.[2]

In a *Boston Globe Magazine* article entitled "Bards at Bat," Thomas P. McDonnell asserts that it has been "left to authentic poets to recognize baseball as something that has to do with the shaping of American myths" (28). In a *New York Times* feature article, Ken Burns, perhaps in a warm-up for his television documentary on baseball in America, refers to the game as "a kind of Rosetta stone of American history and American myth, wherein the lie is as important and certainly as revealing as the truth." Clearly many of the poets who write about baseball choose to go beyond the statistics and time-lapse word photography that would satisfy the historian to construct what could be described as myths about baseball and ourselves.

The purest expression of myth in baseball poetry occurs in William Heyen's "The Stadium," and Phillip Dacey's "Mystery Baseball." The former envisions a potential apocalypse, augured by three nights during which the "moon / has not appeared as even a thin sickle." Consequently, the speaker has gathered with many others to fill the stadium where baseball and religion fuse in propitiatory rituals: "children run the bases;" devotees light candles, chant hymns, and take communion at "the makeshift ... rails / that line the infield grass." Expressing the primary certitude of a true believer, the speaker declares,

> We've known all our lives,
> that we would gather here in the stadium
> on just such a night,
>
> that even the bravest among us

would weep softly in the dark aisles
catching their difficult breath.

[The Host, 27]

Even without Heyen's reference to the children it would be obvious that
the stadium is used here not merely to accommodate large numbers of
worshipers. The crowd's foreknowledge and sense of inevitability suggest that the stadium is not only a suitable place for worship, but that,
given the eschatological circumstances, it is in some way a more appropriate venue than the churches we would normally expect to house such
rituals. The poem takes on added resonance in the light of the commemorative services held in Yankee Stadium following the terrorist
attack on the World Trade Center on September 11, 2001. Given the great
deal of attention writers have paid to the connection between sport and
religion, especially in the last two decades, Heyen's setting for what seem
to be humanity's last rites is wholly appropriate. It is important to note,
however, that Heyen's liturgy excludes references to any sport other than
baseball.

While "The Stadium" conflates established Christian ritual with
baseball, Phillip Dacey in "Mystery Baseball" reaches for a deeper level
of resonance, imbuing the game itself with secrets and riddles which
bring it very close to a religion in and of itself, what Candelaria refers
to as "aboriginal myth and ritual" which give it "a depth of cultural substance similar to that found in other mythologies and human customs"
(13). Dacey's poem reads like a compact Gabriel Garcia Marquez novel:
the season's first pitch is thrown out, not by the president, but by a shadowy figure whose "face has never appeared in newspapers" except as part
of a crowd and it is always blurred; every team fields an invisible player
who wanders the field and taps runners on the shoulder or whispers in
a batter's ear "vague, dark / rumors of his wife," causing the batter to
lose concentration and strike out; pitchers read signs "everywhere"; vendors sell mysterious, unmarked packages, not knowing the contents
themselves, yet fans buy them, "hoping"; a player rounds third base and
disappears; an outfielder ascends while going for a fly ball and is discovered days later, "wandering dazed" in the outfield; finally, an old man
to whom the players pay homage is described as living "deep under second base" (*The Boy*, 7). Dacey's transformation of baseball into aboriginal

myth takes two forms. On the one hand, he takes the ordinary details of the game, a public figure's throwing out the first pitch, a pitcher's searching for signs, a batter's striking out, a runner's being caught off base, and gives them bizarre interpretations calculated to enhance the mysterious qualities of the game. He also invents extraordinary incidents (the ascension and disappearance), and characters (the spirit of the place residing under second base), all of which help Dacey to bypass the game's real history, even its folk mythology, to establish its roots in primitive mythology which predates and subsumes contemporary religions.

Other poets emphasize the humor that is so much a part of baseball, comic characters and situations, but especially the verbal humor, the product of the long hours baseball players spend with their teammates in dugouts or on benches while their team is at bat. While Kinsella is correct to identify baseball as a "game of silences," it is also, perhaps as a direct consequence of those silences (which are dictated by distance and separation rather than rules or etiquette as they are in golf), our most social, conversational game. No sport offers as much social interaction while the game is being played. Verbal play sharpens awareness of language in general, which, in the hands of poets, leads almost inevitably to the linking of baseball and poetry.

Fred Chappell refers to his pitcher in "Spitballer" as a poet, "because his hand goes first / to his head & then to his heart." Chappell says that the catcher "soaks up the curve like / cornflakes in milk," and that the batter hams it up by "wringing out his bat." Everyone knows the wet ball is being thrown, but when the umpire examines it, the ball is "magically dry as alum." The poem is replete with the kind of hyperbole and figurative language that ballplayers delight in. Its climax, too, the observation that the hurler draws a double salary, "Since while he pitches he waters the lawn" (*The World*, 50) succeeds not because it is strikingly original, but because it is so apt, so right, so perfect in capturing the patois of the dugout. "Junk Ball," also by Chappell, relies equally on hyperbole and dugout similes to describe the pitch that takes so long to arrive at the plate it becomes infested with "weevils and termites." Trying to make contact with the garbage pitch is like "Trying to hit Wednesday with a bb gun. / Sunday." It "curves like a Chippendale leg," "flutters" like unsprocketed film, "plunges like Zsa Zsa's neckline," or it sails away "as coy as Shirley Temple." The references to Zsa Zsa and Shirley Temple not only reinforce the feel of the dugout in this poem, but they also suggest '40s and early '50s ambiance which is reinforced by Chappell's conclusion. So slow and circuitous is the flight of the junk ball that "Not even Mussolini could make / the sonafabitch arrive on time" (*The World*, 51).

Dabney Stuart looks at the junk ball from the batter's point of view in "Full Count," in which he pushes baseball myth to the brink of magic realism. Twice in the poem, in fact, Stuart draws attention to his construction of an alternative reality. His epigraph quotes a television documentary on baseball which asserted that "Reality is what the rest of life is all about." Then his speaker, at bat with a full count, must endure a "blind" umpire and a pitcher who is "throwing tin cups." The ball wavers and dips, sails and teeters, and "not one of them" comes "straight or true" or curves predictably. In this situation, "A knuckleball would be a Godsend." Handling each deceptive offering is "like believing / stories about the world / *are* the world" [italics mine].

When the batter fouls "*everything* off" [italics mine], the game is stalled. Theoretically it could go on forever, stuck in this pitcher/batter confrontation. Realizing this, "the catcher finally curls / up for a nap at the umpire's feet," and the umpire, (who is "blind"), thinks the catcher is his dog and that he's back on his own porch relaxing. He "lights his pipe, / tilts, releases," and begins a story with, "Once upon a time." Since the umpire's word is law, the game is suspended, but the players, managers and spectators gather on the field to listen to the story. The pitcher and batter share cool water from a dipper. The story

> goes on
> past suppertime, past the arclights'
> eventual sudden
> blaze into the dark.
> No one tires, or tries
> to predict what will happen next.
> [*Hummers*, 107]

The umpire's tale continues "through mornings of unbearable / loveliness," and could conceivably go on forever, yet no one seems to mind, even after their supply of water and tobacco has been depleted. The speaker cannot predict when the end might come, but he vows that when it does, everyone will have remained quietly on the field at the feet of the storyteller, "settled / into the voice of our calling" (107).

Where Francis and Wallace slow time in order to focus on the details of the plays they are depicting, Stuart manages to halt the passage of time altogether, or at least to defer its effects, by having his batter "foul everything off," thus extending the inning indefinitely. The umpire then turns back the clock, reconciling opposing players and uniting them with the spectators as children enthralled by the umpire's archetypal fairy tale ("once upon a time"). The tale's harmonizing influence is inescapable: "no one argues," "the managers shake hands," the pitcher and batter share a dipper of water, the crowd drifts onto the field and "sits amiably." And though time seems to pass— the lights come on on the field, and by implication are turned off as morning approaches, and several mornings are involved — its effects are not manifested in the participants. No one grows weary or bemoans the lack of cigarettes or water. The possibility of closure (with its consequent resumption of time's effects) is recognized, but understated in comparison with the speaker's authoritative commitment to the protracted moment, the declaration that "whenever the end comes / we *will* still be here, settled / into the voice of our calling" (107).

"Full Count" illustrates what Christian Messenger calls "baseball's seductive promises," the possibility of "return," and "the defeat of mortality" (329). Stuart's epigraph, establishing baseball as an alternative to reality, the batter's reference to accepting illusion for reality, and the umpire's captivating fiction combine to reject those promises, however, by insisting on the illusory nature of the game. We might pretend to stop time in baseball, but the game itself is interrupted in favor of the more affective illusion, the oneiric tales of childhood. The poem thus provides a perfect example of the way in which "play may be seen as the basis for sport but also as its implied opposite and critic in many ways" (Messenger, 11). In one sense, the pitcher's and batter's competition merges with play. The pitcher throws "tin cups" and the batter fouls off everything, thus bringing the game as a series of events in time effectively to a halt. At this point, pure play, with both players and spectators transformed into children, takes over, postponing the resumption of competition for some indefinite future. It is also important to note that all three fictions in Stuart's poem — baseball's, the batter's, and the umpire's — are subsumed under the more comprehensive fiction of the poem itself. "Full Count" thus becomes a self-reflexive endeavor, "an example of the creative process giving phenomonological evidence of itself" (Hassan, 161).

The significant themes of "Full Count" — what Messenger, relying on Derrida, has called "the play back to origins" (10), the notion of the poem as a repository of memories, and the poem as self-reflexive instrument — constitute the driving impulses behind most baseball poetry which goes beyond the imaginative recording of the game's details. They merge in varying degrees of emphasis and proportion through works of almost pure nostalgia, to the numerous evocations of father-son interaction, and emerge in their most telling combination in those poems which look to childhood baseball as a source of the poet's identity as both player and poet.

Nostalgia permeates most baseball poetry, and the more one understands about nostalgia the more appropriate the relationship becomes. Baseball and nostalgia share the same goal — returning home. Nostalgia, from the Greek *nostros*— to return home — and *algia*— a painful condition — literally means "a painful yearning to return home" (Davis 1). But "merely to remember the places of our youth is not the same as to feel nostalgic over them" (Davis, 13). Fred Davis in *Yearning for Yesterday: A Sociology of Nostalgia* argues that "the past which is the object of nostalgia must in some fashion be a personally experienced past rather than one drawn solely, for example, from chronicles, almanacs, history books, memorial tablets, or, for that matter, legend" (8). Moreover, it demands an awareness of the present as a foil to our reconstruction of the past: "the nostalgic evocation of some past state of affairs always occurs in the context of present fears, discontents, anxieties, or uncertainties, even though they may not be in the forefront of awareness" (34–35). Davis identifies three kinds of nostalgia, all of which are common in the poetry of baseball: simple nostalgia, an unchallenged assertion of the past's beauty as compared to the unattractive present; reflexive nostalgia, in which memories of the past are questioned concerning the "truth, accuracy, completeness, or representativeness of the nostalgic claim"; and interpreted nostalgia, wherein a person moves beyond questions of verisimilitude to questions about the act of memory itself. In this mode he asks, "Why am I now feeling nostalgic? What may this mean for my past, for my now? Is it that I am likely to feel nostalgia at certain times and places and not others?" (24). Finally, and this may be for our purposes nostalgia's most significant function, it "is one of the means ... we employ in the never-ending work of constructing, maintaining, and reconstructing our identities" (31).

Though most poems which evoke nostalgia about baseball are first-person memoirs, both Neal Bowers's "Late Innings" and Jonathan Holden's "How to Play Night Baseball" are third-person, lyrical accounts of games which, in Goldstein's words, express the "simultaneous thingness and mystery, fact and emotion" (418) of baseball. Bowers describes boys in a "field across the road," but at a distance in the gathering darkness. His close attention to detail, and his ability to enter the players' minds, suggest he is writing from experience as well as observation. While not as deliberately mythical as "Mystery Baseball," "Late Innings" infuses its own sense of mystery and wonder into the childhood game. The boys are chasing "something so hard to see / it might be imaginary," if not for the smack of the ball against the bat, and as darkness encroaches on the field, they crouch at the plate for the "pitch coming out of nowhere." But Bowers's poem is best at evoking childhood's efforts at prolonging itself by protracting a moment of magic, as the "last boy digs in at home with the crickets, / the gathering dew, waiting for the long, dark curve" (*Helicon Nine*, 19, 45). Though Bowers's speaker never evaluates or judges the situation his lines describe, his tone is nevertheless nostalgic, almost elegiac. When he says that the boys play in "the drained light of a sun already set," he creates the sense of a comparative present that Davis makes essential for true nostalgia, and the "drained light" might very well be a metonym for his own situation. The light he sheds on the darkening scene is that of an adult looking back on and reenvisioning his own childhood in the manner of Seamus Heaney.

Jonathan Holden's "How to Play Night Baseball" is remarkably similar to Bowers's poem, but rather than describing a specific scene, Holden offers a propaedeutic formula for the perfect late evening game, a recipe for the ultimate childhood experience undoubtedly based upon his own playing days. Among the basic elements of such a game are: a "freshly-mown" pasture (not the manicured Little League field), so that the ball will be "bruised with green kisses" when it is hit through the grass; sunburned players, smelling of chlorine; girls in the bleachers, and heat lightning illuminating the western sky. Given these conditions the players must play until the ball is barely visible, "khaki — / a movable piece of twilight," and they "can only see pop-ups, / and routine grounders get lost in / the sweet grass for extra bases" (*Design*, 32). Clearly this is a poem that aims at essence rather than execution. The quality of the play, the feeling derived from it, overcomes the competitive spirit. Holden's poem, more than any other, illustrates Hall's claim that baseball poems allow us to return to childhood, to that "green island in a sea of change" (62) — change, by the way, which is ironically evoked by its absence from the poem. Conspicuously absent from Holden's perfect game are all the contemporary accouterments of modern, suburban youth baseball — lights (it *is* night baseball), uniforms, a manicured field, and umpires.

Both "Late Innings" and "How to Play Night Baseball" are idealized visions of youth or childhood, visions brought on perhaps by the shadowy setting in each piece. Both ignore certain realities that anyone who has played baseball in similar circumstances could, when pressed, recall: mosquitoes, gashes which frequently resulted from sliding into "makeshift bases of tin and cardboard," twisted ankles from stumbling over rough ground in the outfield, angry mothers wanting their children home on time for dinner, and the heartbreak so often linked to those girls Holden describes sitting with bared arms in the bleachers. All the poem's elements make for full-blown nostalgia which is

> neither illusion nor repetition; it is a return to something we never had. And yet the very force of it is just that in it the lost is recognized, is familiar. Through nostalgia we know not only what we hold most dear, but the quality of experiencing that we deny ourselves habitually. This is why nostalgia is a moral sentiment. It is also the moral sentiment of the present century [Harper, 27].

In other words, by choosing to enhance certain aspects of our past we make value judgments which define who we are by revealing what we wish to retain from what was in comparison with what is.

Surprisingly, few baseball poems offer nostalgic portraits of the character who has been a staple of sports literature since Homer — the washed-up jock. Heyen's Mantle sells out, and Corso's Ted Williams, although a failure, is not a shadow of his former self but the cocky, defiant Red Sox hitter in his prime. Donald Petersen's Yankee heroes are all dead. Only Rodney Torreson in "Two Years Retired, Bobby Murcer Makes a Comeback Bid, 1985" and Donald Hall in "Couplet" depict over-the-hill players who, like Nestor, must give in to "gloomy old age." Murcer goes one-for-twelve in a comeback effort that Torreson labels as "a rain dance / in the season of old bones" (*Aethlon* 4.1, 180). Hall describes Ted Williams in an old timers' game at Fenway Park, "laboring" like a crippled dray horse to barely catch a fly ball. Because we remember his youthful body we weep while we applaud his awkward play. Rather than focus on Williams's ineptitude, Hall apotheosizes him, elevating him to the pantheon of all those whose ruin we observe, in the same way that Ulysses wept when he encountered Achilles's shade in the underworld (*Fathers*, 143). Perhaps the relatively few baseball poems centering around the "washed-up jock" can be accounted for by the sense of renewal built into the game itself, the return home which is the goal of every batter, and spring training which ties the game to the natural cycle. Even faded heroes motivate youngsters and rookies, directing attention away from themselves and toward the future, creating an institutional immortality in the way that a father ensures a kind of serial immortality by teaching his son the rudiments of the game.

An entire sub-category of baseball poetry is made up of poems that explore the relationship between fathers and sons, and, with increasing frequency, fathers and daughters. Roger Kahn argues, in fact, that baseball "begins with sons and fathers, fathers and sons. The theme is older than the English novel, older than *Hamlet*, old at least as the *Torah*. You play baseball with love and you play baseball to win and you play baseball with terror, but always against that backdrop, fathers and sons" (5). Donald Hall calls his collection of "Essays on Sport (Mostly Baseball)" *Fathers Playing Catch with Sons*. Both men conjure up visions of fathers and sons indulging in pure play during which deep bonds that will sustain the relationship throughout the years are forged. In reality, and in the poetry about that reality, situations are more complex.

In Judy Goldman's "Suicide," for example, a man about to take his own life spends the afternoon playing catch with his son. "You threw the ball for hours," she writes,

> as if there were no chance
> night would ever search the corners
> like the crowd
> finding places in the stands,
> their eyes marking the hard mound of dirt
> below. For hours.
> As if there were nothing at all
> left to explain.
>
> [*Holding Back Winter*, 45]

Goldman's closing lines, with their emphasis on the suicide's prolongation of the game with his son, suggest that the simple tossing of the ball staved off the darkness for as long as possible, was the most meaningful endeavor the father could have taken on in his last hours, and in effect functioned as an explanation of sorts to his son. The fact remains, however, that it wasn't enough to prevent him from taking his life, and one wonders what memories will be evoked for the boy when he encounters fathers playing catch with sons in any context.

Often women bring to sports poetry the perspective of passionate outsiders capable of the insight only those who have been essentially ignored can bring us. I explore this notion in more depth in the chapter on women's poetry about sport. Here I wish to cite just one more brief example of a rigorously anti-nostalgic father/child baseball poem. In Linda Mizejewski's "Season Wish" a woman looks back on her father's efforts to transform her into a boy by taking her each spring "out at dusk / to lots the boys had left" where he would test her each year to see if she could throw "the winning curve back at him / and learn to catch," adopt "the grip and swing / of a missing son." He hoped to mute her femininity by tucking her hair up under her cap, retard the growth of her breasts with the glove pressed close to her chest, thicken her wrists with practice until she looked like a boy. Failing this transformation, the father switched tactics, used her as bait, sweetened by a legacy of investments and the family business, to entice a prospective husband, "a man who might / try to be a son" (*Hummers*, 81). The schemes always failed and the daughter returned "still a girl," while the father returned each

49

spring to the stones he piled up for bases in the empty lot, where he would kneel in the dirt, as if in prayer, trying to effect his own form of alchemy. The ball games the father and daughter engaged in in "Season Wish" are obviously a perverse kind of training rather than play, and the legacy the father's "care" passed on was one of unrelieved bitterness.

Conrad Hilberry's "Instruction," on the other hand, proudly describes a transformation of a young girl into a baseball player who adopts decidedly male mannerisms. The speaker's daughter has learned the fundamentals—running, catching, throwing off her mask—from her coach. "*On her own*," [my italics] however, she learns such "male" nuances as "how to knock the dirt out of her cleats, / hitch up her pants," to spit so that she just misses her shoulder, and to "stare incredulously at the ump" (*Hummers*, 46). Critical here is the notion that the young girl willingly and actively studies the posturing of more experienced players not so much in order to be "one of the guys," but to establish her own credibility and authority as an insider in the complete sense of the word.

In "Instruction" the father's role is neither as coach nor overweening parent, but as observer pleased at his child's initiative and developing independence. Other father/child poems with baseball as their matrix include Charles B. Wheeler's "Going to the Ballgame" and Lawrence Lieberman's "My Father Dreams of Baseball," neither of which fits the pattern of the loving-mentor/eager-novice relationship. In each poem the attitude of the poet/son toward the father is, at best, ambiguous. In Wheeler's piece, the speaker recalls accompanying his father to a Class D baseball game in Arkansas sometime in the thirties. The boy, who seems to be six or eight years of age, is more or less bewildered by the game and the hearty repartee his father engages in with other men in the stands. He also is distanced from the game owing to poor eyesight. He mentions, in fact, that he had not yet started to wear glasses. Rather than a warm reminiscence, the poem becomes a study in disaffection. The boy "didn't understand" much of the bleacher banter, and apparently couldn't fathom the intricacies of the scorecard either. He says his father "tried to show me / How you marked it," but never says the father's efforts succeeded. Worse, the father's comments about the game make him "ill at ease." He recognizes, moreover, that the father, who had lettered in all sports in college,

>   couldn't wisecrack the way
>   Other men in the stands could,
>   With self-satisfied guffaws
>   At especially telling points,
>   Making a ragged little drama
>   That counterpointed the ballgame,
>   But he shouted a lot and got mad
>
>   ....
>   [*Aethlon*, 7.2, 122]

The speaker admits that he "lived for the seventh inning," a soft drink and a stretch to ease "the stiffness," a term that applies to the relationship as well as his physical condition. When the father asks him how he liked the game he says, "I couldn't tell him, but I answered somehow. / I still don't know" (123). After the game the two silently ride home, where the boy once more is excluded as he lies in bed listening to his parents talk "a long time in the bedroom" (124). The boy, who describes himself as "certain of my irrelevance," sleeps, and the next morning after breakfast the father goes off to work. The game is never discussed.

Older, Wheeler obviously takes advantage of readers' expectations about the closeness of the father/son baseball experience to establish a poignant contrast between those expectations and the very real sense of loneliness and irrelevance his speaker suffered as a child. But while Wheeler uses the father/son excursion to the ballpark to accentuate the boy's relative isolation, Lawrence Lieberman in "My Father Dreams of Baseball" suggests an even deeper isolation by failing to mention himself at all. Admittedly, Lieberman focuses on the father and the powerful contrast between his dreams of heroic, idealized baseball, and the ugly reality of the father's angry reactions (presumably at an earlier age) to games he had bet on heavily, and the father was a sore loser. Lieberman formally underscores this contrast by describing the ideal (current) dreams of the older man in three stanzas set against the left margin. Interspersed among these are three stanzas dealing with the younger, more aggressive gambler. The dreamer conjures up long home runs, dazzling caps, and spectacular catches by players whose features are fixed in the father's mind like ancient faces, "cast in bronze or brass."

Set against these dreams is the portrait of a man who storms out of the house when his team loses, rants at the umpire and heads out in his Porsche for a night of drinking. The next morning, Lieberman writes, "mother's throat has a telltale lump," meaning, I think, not that the father struck the mother, but that she had difficulty explaining the father's behavior to the son. When the father actually attends games, he assumes the character of a matador at the bullfights, directing the picador pitchers to "kill" the heavy hitters with their curve ball lances (*Unblinding*, 19).

Point of view is everything in "My Father Dreams...." Both time frames, delivered in the present tense, are clearly in the speaker's mind, yet he deliberately excludes himself as an actor from the poem. If, as a boy, he had attended the games with his father at all, his failure to register his own reactions is as telling as if he had described them fully. Only now, as an adult, can he "forgive" the father by reconciling his earlier behavior with the idealized vision of the present. That he "allows" the father's visionary claims is evident from his surrounding the real with the ideal in the poem which begins with imagined home runs and closes with the sculptural image of the hero.

Father/child baseball poems which more nearly fulfill the expectations Kahn's and Hall's comments generate include Quincy Troupe's "Poem for My Father," Ron Smith's "Striking Out My Son in the Father-Son Game," Doug Carlson's "Russ Joy Little League," David Bottoms's "Sign for My Father, Who Stressed the Bunt," and Jack Ridl's "Good Training for Poetry." Troupe's "Poem for My Father" celebrates "the glory of great black men" who played in the Negro Leagues, one of whom was Quincy T. Troupe, Sr., a catcher. Not only does the poem express the son's pride in his father's athletic accomplishments, it elevates the father to a pantheon of African-American sports heroes which includes Satchel Paige, "Cool Papa" Bell, Josh Gibson, and Joe Louis, all harbingers of cultural "shock waves, soon come" (*Avalanche*, 82). Ron Smith's poem describes a man pitching for the fathers against their sons' team. Despite his obvious love for his son, and his anxiety about the boy's performance, the man cannot restrain his own competitive urge, and so strikes out the boy his first time at bat. What's worse is that he knows, his wife's glare from the bleachers notwithstanding, that he will strike the boy out his next time at bat as well. "These little boys," he says, "will never hit me today" (*Running*, 52). New age, non-competitive critics might read Smith's poem as a condemnation of the competitive spirit, the father bullying the son. The poet understands the man's foolishness, however, and knows that the boys will, in effect, win by bringing their fathers down to their level.

In "Russ Joy Little League" a father empathizes with his son who is batting with two outs and two strikes in the last inning with a runner on second. He tries to see the game as simple play, twice saying, "I'm trying not to be competitive," but can't resist his desire for the boy to be the hero and perhaps compensate for his own sense of inadequacy. He tells his son, for example, "you / are two-for-two; I am oh-for-thirty-seven." The poem ends without revealing the boy's fate, but the father looks forward to less stressful times together. He writes:

> Now I want to be with you
> in our fantasies: a compact, level
> swing, the ball sailing like a gull
> out and over the falling sun
> to a jetty where we sit growing older,
> not competing with fish we never catch.
> [*I Hate Long Goodbyes*, 17]

The father's love for the son is fully evident, and his looking forward to "a relatively distant point in the future" at which time man and boy could look back "nostalgically on events that were imminent or whose occurrence could be anticipated" illustrates perfectly the strange phenomenon Davis identifies as "nostalgia for the future" (12).

The poem that most completely satisfies the common perception of a father/son baseball poem is David Bottoms's "Sign for My Father, Who Stressed the Bunt." Bottoms recalls his father teaching him techniques for bunting on "the hand-cut field below the dog lot and barn." But like all boys, he could not take his eyes "off the bank / that served as our center-field fence." Through all his years of organized baseball, the son swung for the fences, the father all the while stressing "the same technique," the critical fundamentals that never change. But Bottoms admits he "never learned" what the father was "laying down" (*Armored Hearts*, 39). Only now as an adult, as a poet, can he begin to recognize the value of the father's patient teaching, not only for baseball, but for life itself, for the writing of poetry. Bottoms's poem does not reiterate the much-abused baseball-is-life analogy. The lessons the father teaches the son apply directly to baseball. They stand for nothing else. They are, however, a part of the poet's experience whose lessons may be applied to life at large and thus function synecdochically rather than metaphorically.

Jack Ridl comes much closer to the baseball/life metaphor in his father/child baseball poem, "Good Training for Poetry." Ridl adds a dimension to the usual two-generation approach by positioning himself between his ball-playing daughter and his own father who is a golfer. He recalls the pride he felt when he homered his first time at bat in college baseball, his father saying, "Thanks," and slapping his hand as he rounded third base. But the home run, his only one, was a false promise. He ultimately lost his eye and ended his college career unable to "hit a cantaloupe with a tennis racquet." Virtually haunted by his failure to live up to his own and his father's expectations, he now watches his daughter "take her cuts," and sees his father sink "five out of seven" twelve foot putts, still feeling the slap of the father's hand, wondering why he, the son, "ended / like a blind man / on the bench, a daughter / dashing home from first, / a father dropping out of sight" (*Between*, 15).

The "good training for poetry" is apparently Ridl's struggle to reconcile himself to the unheroic life, and the task of balancing his joy in his daughter's success (and the hard-earned knowledge that he cannot let his own ambition rule her life), with the prospect of his own father's decline. By implying that resignation, knowledge, love and sadness are prerequisites for the poet, Ridl further strengthens the parallel between baseball and writing articulated in Mike Shannon's "The Art of Baseball Poetry" and first made explicit in Marianne Moore's "Baseball and Writing."

Many of the poems discussed between Shannon's and Ridl's have made direct or oblique references to the baseball/writing parallel. Wheeler's "Going to the Ballgame" begins, "'PEEnuts, POP-CORN, CRACKerjax!' / A trochee, a spondee, and a dactyl" (*Aethlon* 7.2, 122), designations only the discriminating ear of the adult poet could make. David Bottoms's "Sign for My Father..." stresses the connection when Bottoms writes, "let this be a sign," "this" meaning the poem itself which becomes one more example of the poem calling attention to itself as artifact.

I. "Who the Hell Are You, Kid?"

It is almost axiomatic that writing about games and play is writing about writing. Nowhere is this self-reflexive tendency more evident than in poems about baseball. These poems emphasize language: as a product of the game itself (in which case one's identity as a player is equated with his ability to use the language appropriate to the game); as a record of the poet's reflection upon the creative process—the degree to which play on the field encourages play with words, the reliability of language as a vehicle for recording events and memories, and the credibility of memory itself.

Baseball poetry adopts the language of the game to a degree unsurpassed by poetry about any other sport. I refer here not so much to the technical jargon of the experts, but to the language the players themselves use to identify each other as members of the fraternity. In Gary Gildner's "In My Meanest Daydream" the speaker dreams of aggressively pitching to a dangerous hitter, "shaving / letters, dusting off / the heavy sticker crowding clean-up / clean down to his smelly socks." He and the catcher communicate almost unconsciously and everything is working, so well that he lets fly a stream of spit and the catcher "pops his mitt / & grins / & calls me baby" (*Warsaw Sparks*, 115). In "Speaking in Tongues" Gildner describes the difficulty of explaining what he as a coach expects of his Polish baseball players who have only a vague notion of the game. Gildner asks his translator to tell his Warsaw Sparks, "…the ball is / part of them, their arms, their souls— / it should travel true and beautiful. / They're moving like the devil's / got their peckers packed in ice." When his translator tells the coach his sentiments are difficult to convey, Gildner tries another tack, explaining that God has a passionate interest in baseball and that he is "hungry for a Warsaw win." The image of God as a cosmic coach gets through, and George, the translator, begins "talking turkey … passing on the word… / and my guys are trying hard to catch / the lingo and the rhythm" (*Warsaw Sparks*, 56–57). It is almost as if language and play are equated, that the language must be mastered before the skill in the game itself can evolve.

Jonathan Holden's "Hitting Against Mike Cutler" reverses the situation of Gildner's "In My Meanest Daydream." Holden's speaker is the hitter, facing a pitcher who looks to him like a gunslinger in a shooting gallery. The catcher "clucks contentedly" behind the plate, and when the pitch burns by the batter like a hornet, "hisses, vanishes with a

BANG. STEE-RIKE! / The catcher grins. Good chuck, good chuck, he clucks" (*Design*, 32). Here in his onomatopoetic ending it almost seems as if Holden loses faith in his ability to describe what happens through the semantic content of his words. He, in effect, allows the sounds and rhythms of the game to speak for him.

In "How I Learned English" Gregory Djanikian's immigrant speaker is assimilated into the team and is well on his way to becoming "naturalized" once he learns the language of the sandlot. Thrown into a pickup game in his new home, striking out regularly and "banished to the outfield," he longs for his homeland and wonders if he will always be an alien. But when he is hit in the head by a fly ball he falls back, clutches his brow, and exclaims, because he knows no better, "Oh my shin, oh my shin." His malapropism breaks the ice and the entire team falls to the ground around him seized by paroxysms of laughter, calling out "shin" again when the laughter begins to fade. Despite his injury the "new boy"

> played on till dusk
> Missing flies and pop-ups and grounders
> And calling out in desperation things like
> "Yours" and "take it," but doing all right,
> Tugging at my cap in just the right way,
> Crouching low, my feet set,
> "Hum baby," sweetly on my lips.
> [*Falling Deeply*, 30]

Language takes precedence over performance. Saying the right words identifies the speaker as player and facilitates his assimilation into the culture.

Two poems stand out more than any others as examples of the equation of writing and playing baseball. It is not coincidental that both focus on the pitcher as poet, since the pitcher controls the rhythm and shape of the game (the catcher's signals notwithstanding). He is the *auteur* who leaves his mark on the box scores. "His art is eccentricity," as Robert Francis explains in "Pitcher." His purpose is to "communicate," but to make "the batter understand too late" (*Orb Weaver*, 8). Francis's poem is probably the most widely anthologized of all baseball poems and I need not dwell on it in detail here, except to note that the poet's emphasis on art and communication underscores his intention to equate pitcher with poet, and that this poem, like MacLeish's "Ars Poetica" and Mike Shannon's "The Art of Baseball Poetry" almost undermines itself, by insisting on indirection and subtlety in both pitching and art, and thus rather nakedly making the point that is understood, not too late, but almost immediately.

Not as well known, but a more personal and complex declaration of the baseball/writing parallel, is Jonathan Holden's "A Poem for Ed 'Whitey' Ford." The first third of Holden's poem seems to be about pitching and only pitching. His speaker declares his admiration for Ford and his early ambition to model himself after the Yankee pitcher. Like Ford, he wanted to be a finesse player, "a low ball specialist / but sneaky fast, tough / in the clutch" (*Falling from Stardom*, 23). But when Holden writes, "I never wanted to go / soft, to fall in love fall / through it and keep falling like this" (23), the perspective of the poem shifts and the reader comes to understand that Holden's speaker is not looking back on a youthful goal he continues to pursue. Falling in love changed him, forced him to "dwell in this gray / area, this interval where we search out by feel / the seams in the day, / homesick for the warm, / map of a hand" (23).

Before love sidetracked him, he had planned to be as detached and "immune as Ford," with a strict, classic delivery, not

> to sit thinking like this
> how I drive the blunt wedge
> of my breath before me
> one space at a time,
> watching words
> I thought were well meant
> miss.
> [*Falling from Stardom*, 24]

Here, in the speaker's admission of failure, both in his effort to imitate Ford and in his unsuccessful struggle to make each word hit home, the poet/pitcher equation becomes explicit, yet at the same time a contrast between the two "players'" techniques and methods in their respective arts develops. Ironically, the poet's admission of his failure to perform as a writer the way Ford performed on the mound, his inability to "be ice," or "throw uncontradicted strikes," elevates him above his hero. The poet's lot is to dwell in gray areas, to search out and feel "the seams in the day." Love muddles the poet's vision, precludes his being "empty, cruel, accurate." And while both poet and pitcher strive for "expertise," only the pitcher's art can be "pure," unalloyed by the insecurity, empathy, and exuberance that keep poets human.

Though memory-based, Holden's "Poem..." is not a nostalgic vision of a particular game or season but a generalized record of the poet's struggle to overcome the obstacles that emotions throw up in his way during his pursuit of "expertise." His identity as a poet evolves against the backdrop of his ongoing comparison of himself to Ford. Many of the poems examined in this chapter become, at least implicitly, vehicles for the identities of their respective speaker/poets. Other poets who explicitly employ the baseball poem as a vehicle for identity bring together the diverse motifs and themes discussed thus far: the aesthetic element of the game, its potential for myth, its mystery, history, and heroic element, along with the nearly ubiquitous emphasis on language; but for these poets, the primary focus, through memories, is on their own growth and maturation both as players and writers. Their memories engage our memories, and through language reveal what Rosenthal has called "the private relation each person has with the world" (27), thus providing the baseball poem with the fullest expression of its potential as poetry. These poets neither record the artistic performances of abstract players, nor stand in awe of the pin-striped figures on the manicured grass of Yankee Stadium, but recall instead their own experiences on the sandlot or the Little League field. Their heroes are not Nomar Garciaparra, Barry Bonds or Sammy Sosa, but themselves.

I would like to examine five poems as "vehicles for identity": William Matthews's "The Hummer," Richard Hugo's "From Altitude: The Diamonds," Arthur Smith's "Extra Innings," Richard Jackson's "Center Field," and Dave Smith's "The Roundhouse Voices," all five of which reveal what A. Bartlett Giamatti felt were most important to our understanding of baseball — memories of "ourselves at our earliest." But those memories, "now smooth and bending away from us in the interior of ourselves, are not simply of childhood or of a childhood game. They are memories of a time when all that would be better was before us, as a hope, and the hope was fastened to a game" (82). From a sociologist's perspective, Davis agrees, arguing that the goal of the nostalgic experience is "to ensure continuity of identity." But for that continuity to be realized, "some evaluative or appreciative stance toward former selves is required as well" (35), especially when stress and a sense of discontinuity plague our lives. All five of the poems discussed below perform such evaluation.

Of the five, only "The Hummer" lacks a first-person narrator. Still it presents an intimate view of childhood baseball, in this instance a solitary, almost solipsistic, game that is created, played, and umpired by the young boy in the poem who marked a strike zone on the door of a shed and spent the summer trying to hit it with a wet tennis ball which showed him, at least early in his games, the exact location of each pitch.

Better than any piece I know, this poem illustrates the paradox of inconsequence in sport, the notion that games become significant in inverse proportion to their association with the *real* world. The smaller the recognition and tangible reward associated with a particular game, the more significant it becomes *qua* game.

In this instance the game is without significance beyond the confines of the moral framework the boy himself erects and adheres to. But in the later innings, when the door was "solidly blotched,"

> calling the corners was fierce
> enough moral work for any
> man he might grow up to be,
>   [*Selected Poems*, 126]

since he finished any game he started, even if he was losing early on.

So fully is the boy drawn into his creation that he would have been the batter if he could have, "trying to stay alive." This last phrase carries with it the boy's realization that each out implies a death of sorts, one recorded in real games in the box score, "the obituary." Still the youthful pitcher "loved ... mowing them down," as if he felt himself somehow beyond the bounds of mortality. But when it came time to administer the *coup de grace*, "the hummer,"

> it made him grunt to throw it,
> as if he'd tried to hold it
> back, but it escaped. Thwap.
> [126]

The impulse for self-preservation (after all the batter is the boy too) conflicts here with the desire for resolution, but the finality of the poem's last syllable leaves no doubt that each game-winning strikeout pounds one more nail in the coffin of the boy's childhood.

The celebration of the childhood game is shadowed by the mature narrator's recognition that even the difficult, later-inning calls the boy made were simple compared to the complex decisions he would be responsible for in adulthood. This dual vision, a fusion of innocence and experience, is significant in many good poems but it is critical to the effective sports poem, since one of the major themes of all sports literature is loss: loss of ability, loss of perspective, loss of innocence, of life, loss even of our ability to remember events which generated powerful emotions in the first place.

Rather than lamenting the loss of historical accuracy or resorting to the last refuge of statisticians ("You could look it up") the poet capitalizes on the unreliability of memory by freely admitting the creative role of the imagination in reconstructing our childhoods. In the long title poem of *A Happy Childhood*, Matthews says

> There's no truth about your childhood,
> though there's a story, yours to tend
> like a fire or garden.
> [*Selected Poems*, 112]

The poet here engages in what Davis defines as "interpreted nostalgia," and concludes that childhood is, in effect, self-created. As Rollo May writes, "What an individual seeks to become determines what he remembers of his has been" (69). We become what we were, but what we were is not determined until the mature imagination has the capacity to construct what Gaston Bachelard calls "moments of illumination ... moments of poetic existence" (100). Thus, the degree of poignancy associated with the loss of youth is directly proportional to our ability to heighten those moments.

I. "Who the Hell Are You, Kid?"

In "From Altitude: The Diamonds," Richard Hugo's memories of a whole life of baseball are triggered by the ubiquitous baseball diamonds one sees from airplanes flying over this country. In this case, though, the "memories" are a product of wish fulfillment on the part of the speaker. He creates for himself a past in which his baseball triumphs and failures represent the victories and defeats of his life as a whole. Adopting the second-person point of view, Hugo says, "You played on every one," blending observations about his own present state (fat, bald, anxious about flying) with what might be called nostalgic fantasies which, the reader understands, cannot be historically accurate: You "tripled home / the run" to beat the Sox in Chicago; you pitched a great game in the Bronx, ultimately losing to "that left-hander, / Ford, who made it big..." (*Making Certain*, 364).

Hugo's second-person narrator, coupled with the diverse and varied nature of the experiences he describes while flying across the United States, creates an American Everyman who, as his plane descends toward a landing, focuses in upon another ballpark, with runners rounding third, driven home by a triple, the hitter

> his lungs filled with the cheers of those
> he has loved forever, on his magnificent tiny way
> to an easy stand-up three.
>
> [*Making Certain*, 365]

Life goes on. Vitality is renewed in each game on all those highly recognizable diamonds that decorate the landscape.

The imagination's ability to illuminate the past and the contrast between history and the creative memory are the driving impulses of Arthur Smith's "Extra Innings" in which he recalls that the ballpark grass of his youth was so

> sweet-smelling, I think
> I could have bellied down near the dugout
> And drowsed away the afternoon.
>
> [*Elegy*, 10]

Against this background of pastoral innocence he remembers breaking up the no-hitter of a young man who turns out to have been Tom Seaver.

But then the speaker questions the validity of his reminiscence, think-ing that Seaver, looking back, would remember a no-hitter accom-plished, the last out being a strikeout, and that the left fielder might recall saving the game with a shoestring catch for the last out. Smith, like Hugo, asserts that the facts are not as important as our memories, which create our own reality.

> We try to
>   accommodate
> what happened with what
> Might have happened. And it never turns out true,
>
> The possibilities not to be trusted, but rather,
> Believed in against the facts—whatever they are.
>
>   [*Elegy*, 11]

We are the product of our memories of what we were, but we create those memories, those myths of ourselves. Though Tom Seaver appears in "Extra Innings," his role is decidedly unheroic, the impulse of the poem determinedly reductive insofar as the superstar is concerned. Seaver might not even have been the pitcher who opposed the speaker in his youth, and if he had been, his memories of the event would not have carried more weight than those of the speaker, the other possible pitcher or the opposing team's left fielder.

Unlike "The Hummer" or "Extra Innings," Richard Jackson's "Cen-ter Field" is set in the present, but it quickly turns to the past as the speaker waits for a long fly ball to come down. It has been hit into the dusky shadows beyond the field lights and as the speaker waits for it to drop he "worries as his eyes try to focus on the tiny white sphere; his small well-lit portion of the outfield, the world, shrinks in the face of the approaching dusk; suddenly the outfield is uneven, dangerous, per-haps" (Goldstein, 419). He notes that the field makes backpedaling "risky / but keeps pulling you as if further into your past."

As he waits for the ball to materialize out of the darkness Jackson invokes the sandlot in Lawrence, Massachusetts. He muses about "what we try to steal from our darkening pasts,"

> how age means knowing how many steps we have lost,
> remembering that too many friends have died,

and how love is the most important thing,
if only we knew how and when.

[*Worlds Apart*, 16]

The remaining two-thirds of the poem becomes an inventory of losses couched in baseball terms. In reverie the poet has "slid/ over the outstretched arms of twenty years," and "can see Joey Gile crouched at third base" waiting for a sniper's bullet to "snap like a line drive into his chest." Then there was John Kearns who would "swing and miss everything / from a tree in his backyard," and Joe Daly who was "tagged ... to a tree" by a tractor, and Gene Coskren, "fooled by a hit and run in Syracuse." The poet even recalls two aunts, one who loved baseball, a victim of cancer. The other died thinking there was "no one to bring her home."

"Center Field's" final stanza becomes blatantly self-reflexive and establishes the poem as more than a nostalgic collection of puns. Jackson, who has already drawn the reader into the poem with the use of the second person, involves him more deeply by admitting that "this is a poem"

that could go on being about either death or love,
and we have only the uncertain hang time
of a fly ball to decide how to position ourselves,
to find the right words for our love,
to turn towards home as the night falls, as the ball
as the loves, the deaths we grab for our own.

[17]

By inviting the reader into the poem as, in effect, co-creator, Jackson moves one step beyond the assertion of the memory's creative capacity, and, like Matthews, indulges in "interpreted nostalgia." In this stage, the interlocutor asks, "What may this [memory] mean for my past, for my now? ... What does nostalgia serve for me: For others? For the times in which we live?" (Davis, 24). Finding the "right words for our love" means that we rely on our active imaginations to carry us out of the past into a creative present. We become more than what our memories tell us we were. Recognizing the inevitability of loss, we become what we say we will become, the central figures in our own myths, not merely re-living a past but creating a present in response to that past.

In stark contrast to the speaker in "Center Field," Dave Smith in "The Roundhouse Voices" questions the validity of words as a recompense for grief. At one point Smith's speaker bitterly asserts that "words are all we ever were and they did us / no damn good" (*Goshawk, Antelope*, 101). The lines are addressed to an uncle laid out in his casket for burial. A father surrogate, the uncle had taught the speaker as a young boy how to play baseball. Technically, they *played* softball, but references to "the Mick" and taking a "hard pitch" make it clear that the softball was a concession to the boy's inexperience and the unique setting of their games, a railroad line's roundhouse.

Like "Center Field," "The Roundhouse Voices" is replete with baseball terminology, "diamonds," sliding, pinstripes, stealing, etc., but Smith's poem is a narrative and the relationships are more dramatic than in Jackson's piece. Because the game took place in the roundhouse where the uncle worked, the boy had to sneak in, eluding the watchful eyes of the company guard who would pursue him with a question repeated, with slight variations, four times in the poem: "Who the hell are you, kid?" Eluding the guard becomes as much a part of the game, and the lesson for life, as the pitching and the catching, and as the poem develops the guard comes to represent the restrictions and limitations the child will encounter in the adult world: work, the ownership of property, management by arbitrary authority, and, ultimately, death.

With his uncle's encouragement, the boy taunts the guard, giving him the finger, "just to make him get up / and chase me into a dream of scoring at your feet" (100). In his innocence the boy exults in the ritual defeat of repression, is perhaps even lulled into a false sense of security when the guard succumbs to a heart attack, making evasion unnecessary. But as an adult, returned home for his uncle's funeral, he realizes that he learned the wrong lesson from the guard's disability, that even the uncle's instruction was a betrayal of sorts in that it led him to face life too optimistically. "I gave him [the guard] every name in the book, Uncle," the grieving nephew says, "but he caught us / and what good did all those hours of coaching do?" (101).

All that coaching failed to prepare the speaker for the ultimate defeat that death brings. He stands at his uncle's casket, holding the dead man's hand, "trying to say back that life, / to get under that fence with words..." but the gesture is futile, "and even the finger I give death is words / that won't let us be what we wanted," he says. In this instance, even words are "no damn good" (101).

The poem ends with the nephew saying that he has had enough of words and he has brought them back to the uncle's bier

> where the tick and creak of everything dies
> in your tiny starlight and I stand down
> on my knees to cry, *Who the hell are you, kid?*
> [*Goshawk*, 102]

Each time the question is asked in the poem it takes on slightly different meanings. Initially it might have been a legitimate question on the part of the guard, but after repeated encounters with the boy it had to have become essentially rhetorical. The guard would have known the boy's identity and would have meant, in effect, "What are you doing in my life?" In its final iteration the question is certainly genuine. The nephew, disillusioned and needing direction, is uncertain of his own identity. If all the games, all the coaching, all the words were inadequate preparation for life then what could he be? How could he go on?

The questions become more telling in the light of the speaker's assessing the uncle's failure in terms of words, not lessons, not techniques or strategies, but words, the tools of the poet, not the ballplayer. Smith's comment about the poet's raw material in *Local Assays: On Contemporary Poetry* is relevant. He says, "Words are the poet's enemies, conspirators, and only allies" (29). The very nature of the craft forces the poet to struggle against, conspire with, and finally accept as confederates the words that constitute his art. Unlike many post-modern writers, Smith cannot merely throw up his hands in despair, resort to minimalism, or retreat in silence, as other poems in *Goshawk, Antelope* where "The Roundhouse Voices" is collected, make clear. Still, the temporary effect of the uncle's death is to precipitate an identity crisis. The question of how to continue won't disappear.

From one point of view one might argue that the poem itself answers that question, that art's ability to preserve experience, however bleak, is ample recompense for suffering. In this light we might answer the speaker's question by saying, "You're a poet, and this fine poem gives the lie to your assertion that 'words are no damn good.' Your complaint is like Coleridge's claiming in 'Dejection: An Ode' that his imagination has gone dead." Such a resolution would do violence to the poem, however. Unlike "Center Field," "The Roundhouse Voices" is not meant to be even guardedly optimistic. Its speaker is genuinely bewildered, at a loss to understand or explain who or what he is. Resolution, though it is hard-won, comes in other poems in *Goshawk, Antelope*.

More important is the fact that the question arises at all, that the inquiry as to the speaker's identity must be seen against the backdrop of his childhood experiences as a ballplayer. Like Matthews, Arthur Smith, Richard Jackson, and countless other contemporary poets, Dave Smith examines these experiences in an effort to determine their effect on what he has become. Like most contemporary baseball poets he might refer to "the Mick" or another of baseball's immortals, but in his poem, like the others', the real hero is himself.

II

"End-Zones Scored with Darkness"
The Football Poem¹

Since baseball is generally regarded as "the poet's game," and the overwhelming number of baseball poems constitutes a benchmark against which poetry about other team sports must be measured, an examination of the football poem in contemporary American literature should begin with such a measurement. While it is impossible to fully delineate the baseball poem in a few sentences, and no single representative poem exists, five characteristics appear in enough baseball poems for those features to be regarded as basic motifs: history as reflected in records and statistics, anecdotes and myths about the game and its players; a sense of "mystery"; fathers and sons; an emphasis on language; and a pervasive sense of nostalgia. The *ur* baseball poem would be one in which the poet/father plays ball with his son in their suburban backyard and recalls how his own father, a former Brooklyn Dodger with a .302 lifetime batting average, taught him about baseball, about the meanings of "home" and "sacrifice," and life in general in their Kentucky pasture. The speaker realizes that his father's active days are over, and that he himself is slowing down, finding it more difficult to get out of bed the morning after a pickup game, but the boy, the boy has promise!

Football, as it is depicted in our poems, is a different ballgame altogether, and there are more football poems than one might think. Though baseball poems are in the overwhelming majority, Bob Hamblin, in a paper delivered at the Midwest Popular Culture Association meeting, reported that of 136 poems published in the first seven volumes of *Arete/Aethlon*, 25 of them were football poems. Thirty of them dealt with baseball. The proportion has changed somewhat in favor of baseball in subsequent issues, but there is a considerable body of material available for analysis. I have examined nearly 50 football pieces from such well-known poets as Randall Jarrell, James Wright, James Dickey, Dave Smith and Rodney Jones, and such relatively obscure ones as Mike Rainnie, an assistant football coach at Falmouth High School in Massachusetts. My analysis reveals a remarkable consistency throughout these works, a consistency that argues for a rather unsettling perception among poets as to the fundamental nature of the game they are describing.

Unlike baseball, football, according to the poets, is a game with little history. When it does emerge, history resides in the personalities of well-known players or coaches. Even these examples, however, are minimal: Randall Jarrell's "Big Daddy" Lipscomb, Dickey's Vince Lombardi, or Don Welch's Bear Bryant. Not only are there no won-lost records or winning percentages, no pass completion or punting statistics given in this body of poetry, there is not a single recorded score! As might be anticipated, given their neglect of history, football poems also contain very little genuine nostalgia. Messenger, reiterating Kevin Kerrane's assertion that football has no "Casey at the Bat," points out that "football is a sport with little backlog of heroic song and story" (255), essentially no history. "Casey" notwithstanding, football has at least as much history as that illuminated by most contemporary baseball poets whose work focuses as much on the baseball of the '50s and early '60s as on the Ruth-Gehrig era.[2]

Football heroes do exist. Witness Fred Exley's near obsession with Frank Gifford in *A Fan's Notes*. In fact, Murray Ross in "Football Red and Baseball Green" argues that the "fundamental difference" in baseball and football is that football is an "heroic" game while baseball is "pastoral." Clearly Ross has broad cultural distinctions in mind here rather than literary criteria. He goes on to identify baseball with the "comic tradition which insists that its players be above all human; while football, in the heroic mode, asks that its players be more than that" (*Sport: Inside Out*, 718–19). While baseball remains the sport in which players most closely resemble "ordinary people," baseball players' reliance on weight training and body building, and their multi-million-dollar contracts, make it difficult for contemporary fans to regard them as "above all human." Moreover, most sport literature, and certainly the poetry, attempts to reduce even the most heroic figures to ordinary proportions, and if a literary analogue were to be established it would be, where the athletes themselves are concerned, neither heroic nor pastoral, but tragic.

Football also generates memories, the stuff of nostalgia if not history, but more often than not these memories are painful: the leg that "hurts now," a reminder of an injury that occurred "sometime in 1945" in Tom Sheehan's "Saturday Ceremonial" (*Aethlon* 7.2, 41); a father's "dreams of 1956 / and the field goal he missed in the snow," which, his son argues, effectively ended his life in Sherman Alexie's "Sudden Death" (*Aethlon* 6.1, 47); and there are several poems that recall brutalizing coaches or humiliating drills that reign paramount in the memories of ex-football players.

The fullest evocation of nostalgia in a piece about football occurs in a song rather than a poem. "No. 29," written and performed by Steve Earle on his *Exit 0* album, captures small-town American football in five verses almost as fully as H. G. Bissinger's highly acclaimed *Friday Night Lights*. Unabashedly sentimental, given to cliché, and, like most song lyrics, dependent on phrasing for its full effect, "No. 29" succeeds nevertheless, because its narrative is deeply representative and real. The speaker, who has been born and reared in the town he calls his own, takes great pride in the fact that everyone in the town knows his name. He has a good job, despite the fact that the town is depressed, but some nights he cannot resist the urge to return to the days when he was the star scat back of the local football team, complete with cheerleader girlfriend, whom the whole town came to see. In the game against local rival Smithville, however, when the speaker's play was called, "Bubba let his man go," and when the runner cut back he was hit and heard something crack, a sound signaling the end of his football career. We don't know the nature and extent of the injury, but in the next line the ex-running back reveals that the residual effects of the injury have lingered into his adult life.

Now, like athletic hangers-on and boosters throughout this country, the faded star attends all the high school's games with their "cold nights" and "half pints." The current team is a good one, with a shifty tailback whom the speaker occasionally takes out to dinner. Not surprisingly, the young running back has inherited the speaker's jersey number. He, too, is # 29. But unlike Joe Lon Mackey in Harry Crews's *A Feast of Snakes*, who is jealous and angry at having been supplanted by Willard Miller as "Boss Snake" of the Mystic High School Rattlers, this former running back seems, on the surface at least, to be content with having been the hero of a season. Earle's speaker ends his narrative saying that he no longer chases big dreams or grabs for brass rings, since he had enjoyed his own time under the arc lights and is now content with his memories.

The song is more sophisticated than the casual listener might think. Its elliptical nature (we don't know what kind of a job the speaker has, whether he married his cheerleader, or exactly what his injury was) and repeated refrain lend it a folk ballad quality. The career-ending injury to the surrogate father who encourages his "son" to follow in his footsteps in spite of the probability of a similar injury to the boy, is a familiar motif in mainstream football poetry. Earle's point of view is also ambiguous. If his speaker is content with his lot, why does his mind wander back to his glory years? Is the writer sympathetic with his speaker, who, like Updike's Flick Webb in "Ex-Basketball Player," can't escape the gravitational pull of his high school past? Or does he, like Updike, implicitly condemn the booster mentality which perpetuates the myth of adolescent heroism?

If nostalgia receives only limited attention in football poems, the sense of wonder and mystery that pervades so many baseball poems is altogether absent, perhaps because the face-to-face brutality of the game precludes meditation or speculative religiosity. The game is too basic, too fundamental. It "fascinates and appals" us, "obsessively claims its warriors" (Messenger, 256). If, as Michael Oriard suggests, the game allows for "redemption in violence and/or beauty" ("Professional Football as Cultural Myth," 34), the poets who write about it home in almost exclusively on the violence. As Ron Smith says in "Noseguard,"

> For me, [the game is] jammed space
> in an avalanche of helmets,
> dust, the jumbled debris
> of knees, of bodies writhing
> on the earth, gnawed
> cleats eye-high raking

on the columns of leg, elbows
in the air like grenades.

[*Arete* 3.1, 61]

After his shower, flush with the throbbing of bruises and abrasions, he never sees "the dark tunnels I move through," but constantly projects in his mind a vision of

the tailback stuck
in the sudden light
of the missed block,
paralyzed like a rabbit
waiting for the shotgun blast
of my caged face.

[62]

Obsession with the thing itself defies interpretation or spiritualization.

Finally, the motif whose absence most strikingly registers the difference between the football and the baseball poem is fathers and sons. Obviously, fathers and sons appear in football poems, although there are fewer appearances by fathers than one might imagine, but in only two of the works I examined, an untitled piece by J. J. McKenna and Jack Driscoll's "Touch Football," do fathers and sons play together. McKenna's poem is remarkable also in being one of the few football poems that deal with the game (here just passing and catching in the backyard) in a positive light. In the poem the father explains that his son expects him to "pass / answers to him" in the same way that he throws long, spiraling passes across a landscape divesting itself of summer's "clutter." The boy "thoughtlessly" catches a long pass thrown to the "far / corner / of the field," and then sprints away toward some imaginary goal line, "widening the gap" between father and son. The poem ends with the father watching as the boy

jogs back from his long run
grinning and graceful
grown tall
on my

silent
applause.

[*Arete* 4.1,170]

The poem chronicles a transitional moment in the boy's life and registers the father's approval at his son's momentary independence, a foreshadowing of the boy's recognition that some questions have to be arrived at on his own. Father and son play catch, but with the father's tacit admission that answers can't be easily passed on, and his recognition that the boy must, of necessity, widen "the gap" between them. The pass and catch game becomes, then, an object lesson in relationships.

Driscoll's poem darkens the playing field and raises the stakes. In a sandlot father/son game of touch football, the son tackles the father "so hard / he fumbles the light / from his frightened hands" (*Fishing the Backwash*, 64). The boy watches "the evening disappear" into the mouth of the man lying in the autumn grass "like a man asleep," with "his legs stiff and skinny." The imagery accumulates to suggest that the father is not sleeping, but dead. Even the boy's observation that the father looks to be sleeping reinforces rather than dispels this notion, since it's the euphemism we all use to describe those who are indeed dead.

As if to counter this assessment, the father whispers, "'It was only touch'" (64), a comment which should reassure the son, but which apparently has the opposite effect, since, in the last two sections of the poem, the boy seems to record all the evidence he can muster to convince himself that the father is actually dead. He touches the man's lips, which are "blue and dreaming toward the year of his death." The "father's crooked fingers feel like winter" (64). The boy even pulls the hood of the man's sweatshirt over his face to form a makeshift shroud. Kneeling above the supine figure, the boy anticipates the assumption of the father's role when he "put[s] on his broken glasses" (64) and stares at the evening sky.

Only in the poem's final four lines does the boy's motivation for his sudden violence and his morbid tendencies become clear. He says:

I hold his hand tightly on the abandoned field
where this string of losses

> still grips our empty hearts, awakened
> and unable to forgive.
>
> [64]

He apparently blames his father for the bleakness which governs their immediate situation and seems to have pervaded their lives in general. The field is "abandoned." Their hearts are "empty," and they've suffered a "string of losses." Having just "awakened," the boy has struck out in the classic Oedipal conflict and "killed" the father, but although he attempts to see with his father's "eyes," he lacks the maturity that will allow him to forgive.

"Touch," with its interaction between the father and son, and with the son inflicting pain upon the father, is indeed a rarity among football poems. When fathers appear in most football poems they are silent watchers, inactive fans who are nevertheless responsible for sending their sons onto the practice and playing fields in an effort to compensate for their own losses and failures. These include the "ruptured night watchman" and "Polacks nursing long beers," in James Wright's "Autumn Begins in Martin's Ferry, Ohio," "proud fathers," who are nonetheless "ashamed to go home" to their wives who need them. "*Therefore*," [italics mine]

> Their sons grow suicidally beautiful
> At the beginning of October,
> And gallop terribly against each other's bodies.
> [*Collected Poems*, 113]

Wright's "therefore" is a logical connector linking the argument preceding it to the conclusion it announces. The sons "grow suicidally beautiful" *because* of their fathers' real or imagined inadequacies, sacrificing themselves in what Robert Haas describes as "an efficient transmutation of lovelessness into stylized violence" (210). Furthermore, the poem, with its insistence on seasonal determinism (when October begins, this *will* happen), suggests that when these sons become fathers, they too will suffer the compulsion to relinquish their sons to the gridiron, thus reenacting the ritual of autumnal sacrifice rather than the promise of serial immortality offered in many poems about other sports.

Wright's fathers have abrogated their roles as mentors, clearing the way for coaches, surrogate fathers who embody all the atavistic tendencies the real fathers cannot legitimately represent. The presence of so many coaches, most of them portrayed critically, is one of the features which distinguish football poems from all other poems about sports. Other unique characteristics include a seemingly inordinate emphasis on practice rather than play, and the prominence of death as a specter haunting the game. Each of these characteristics has at least been suggested in my comparison between football and baseball poems. A closer examination of some of the best works written about football reveals not only their pervasiveness, but also their combined effectiveness in creating a dispiriting vision of the game as it is viewed by sensitive men, most of whom played the game themselves.

"Head Feint, Forearm, Glory," from Dave Smith's *The Fisherman's Whore*, combines all four of the motifs enumerated above and adds the common equation of football with war. The poem begins with an epigraph from Shotgun Brown, the football coach: "We're dead this year. Nobody's coming back" (*The Fisherman's Whore*, 66). The coach's words are quite literal, however, not the "building year" cliché used so often to temper pre-season optimism. It is 1945, and "The coach's head count is short." Some of his prospective players are pursuing other goals, and "others who could not keep / their heads down doze endlessly in sunlit / fields."

The coach and the speaker's father come into clearer focus in the second stanza:

> Shotgun walks uphill from the invisible fifty
> where my father is digging himself out
> of a hole filled with blood and dust. He
> rises when the coach speaks, stations himself
> dead center on the enemy's goal and begins to bang
> his foot in the hands of my dead uncle,
> lifting shot after unerring shot, his eyes
> then the same flawless scowl my mother hides
> in a dresser drawer, his hair long and slick
> as wet hay on a hillside. He is piston crisp.
>
> [66]

II. "End-Zones Scored with Darkness"

Battlefield and football field coalesce, with Shotgun as the dominant figure capable of effecting the father's resurrection: "He / rises when the coach speaks." It is not wholly clear whether this is the war-haunted gridiron, or the actual battlefield where the spirit of Shotgun Brown looms over the foxholes to urge "his boys" on to victory. It is clear that the father, in the poem's present, is absent from the speaker's life, since his mother hides the 1945 photograph in a dresser drawer.

Though the father is gone, Shotgun, "a man of few words," and a Marine, carries on, and years later inherits the son, who, when challenged to "show me what you are," lines up against his opponent and lashes out with a forearm shiver "like a battle-hardened star in Shotgun's eye, / slaughtering the enemy," thus earning the commendation — "you are your father's son." The son stands in the father's place, with the father's quick feints and dreams of glory. "We have made it," he says. His forearm "aches to kill." Blinded by his youth and enthusiasm, he proclaims, "We will not die this year or any other year though we may / lie down with the dead and cry for glory. It is 1960" (67). These last three words in "Head Feint..." undercut the boy's defiance of death and reveal both his and his father's indebtedness to the real father in the poem, Shotgun Brown. The scrimmage lines of the '60s would be drawn in jungle, and there would be little glory, but Shotgun would be there nevertheless.

In "Where It Begins," a poem about young boys' initiation into the rigors of football, Mark Swanson describes the transition the boys undergo when the coach becomes the dominant male figure in their lives. Running onto the field, awkward in their new growth and baby fat, the new players confront their exasperated coach "who shakes his head/ and sinks to his knees looking skyward," as if seeking divine help. Swanson says that

> These boys will remember their fathers
> standing in the tall grass beyond the endzone.
> ....
> but mostly they'll remember that hook-nosed man
> on his knees, that goddamned whistle, glinting
> around his neck as if to shed new light
> on their hazy world, as if the sound,

75

more like the scream of a madman
than the call of any bird, could conjure grace
and power in an instant.
The stopping and starting, the trying to please —
it doesn't end, ever.

[*Aethlon* 5.2, 12]

Though the poem is not completely unsympathetic — the coach does promote strength and grace — the finality of the ultimate line, with its suggestion that the coach's control will extend beyond the season and throughout the adult lives of these boys, is a chilling thought fully consistent with the argument of Smith's "Head Feint...."

The most famous of all coaches' portraits in poems is undoubtedly Gary Gildner's Clifford Hill in "First Practice." Hill is the epitome of malevolence who is evidently aware that his methods would not be condoned publicly, so he holds practice "under the grade school" (*Blue*, 3) where he won't be seen. His sexism and sadism are made doubly horrid in being inflicted on the youngest of players, and, if we can believe Mark Swanson, those boys run the risk of being tainted for their entire lives.

Two of James Dickey's three poems that deal directly with football feature coaches, one positively, the other, at best, ambiguously, although both reinforce the father/coach equation. In "The Bee" the speaker rescues his son who is blindly running toward "the sheer / Murder of California traffic" after having been stung. He attributes his ability to rouse his middle-aged body into action to the discipline he acquired on the practice field at Clemson under Coach Shag Norton and his assistants. After the rescue, Dickey leads his son into the trees where they might listen

For some tobacco—
mumbling voice in the branches to say "That's
a little better."

[*Poems*, 280]

For, as he explains to the boy, "Dead coaches live in the air," and "in the ear / Like fathers, and *urge* and *urge*." Finally, sitting with the son, Dickey feels the dead hand of the coach on his shoulder, and having evidently won approval for his actions, asserts, "Coach Norton, I am your boy" (280).

In a commentary on "The Bee," Dickey has said, "I realize that football players are looked at as proto-fascist figures. But I have never had anything but the more extreme gratitude for my football coaches" (*Self Interviews*, 171). His admiration and gratitude are tempered by doubt, however, in "For the Death of Lombardi." Although Dickey did not in reality play for Lombardi, and even says Lombardi would have "thrown / Me off the team on my best day," he counts himself among those who "entered the bodies / Of Bart Starr, Donny Anderson, Ray Nitschke" (*Central Motion*, 116), and others, Lombardi's boys. Dickey's vicarious attachment to Lombardi's team extends to his imaginatively accompanying those who have answered the coach's summons and gathered around the bed where the coach lies dying of cancer.

Caught up in the doubt generated by the impending death of the man who preached a gospel of winning, Dickey protests that ordinary people are broken by a constant insistence on victory. "Coach," he asks, "don't you know that some of us were ruined / for life?" He declares:

> Everybody can't win. What of almost all
> of us, Vince? We lost.
> And our greatest loss was that we could not survive
> Football.
> [117]

After cataloguing many of the undesirable traits coaches encourage in players, "aggression, meanness, deception, delight in giving / Pain to others," Dickey ends the penultimate section of the poem with another series of questions:

> Did you make of us, indeed,
> Figments overspecialized, brutal ghosts
> Who could have been real
> Men in a better sense? Have you driven us mad
> Over nothing? Does your death set us free?
> [117]

Yes and no. Surrounded by the spectral detritus of years spent in locker rooms and training bays, Dickey is forced to admit, even in the face of overwhelming physical evidence, that "there's such a thing / As winning" (117). But it's Lombardi's dignity and resignation as a human being that wins here, his genuine character which emerges through his losing the ultimate battle.

As David Vanderwerken makes clear in his comprehensive analysis of "For the Death...," "the human voice, ordered by the imagination, has the last word" in the poem (141). It is significant that in the final two lines of the piece, the "Coach" has disappeared, and when Dickey asserts that, "We're with you all the way," he addresses the man with whom he can finally identify. "You're going forever, Vince" (118), Dickey writes in the last line, underscoring that identification by using Lombardi's given name, not "Coach," or "Mr. Lombardi," the form of address even those players closest to him were encouraged to use. The point, in my opinion, is that the human example outweighs all the exhortation, the preaching, the driving of an entire career in coaching. What Lombardi ultimately teaches us is, as Vanderwerken says, "how to die" (142).

A further "softening" of the portraits of football coaches occurs in Don Welch's "To Bear Bryant, Somewhere On That Taller Tower." Like Dickey's this one is also a eulogy, with the "taller tower" signifying the deceased coach's heavenly perspective. After establishing his own stance early in the poem — "the most important rivers run out of / the smallest glands in our lives" — Welch describes a neighbor boy and his dog playing next door. It is a beautiful spring day which reminds the poet of the words of another "old coach," William Carlos Williams, "No ideas / but in things." He goes on to catalogue the "things" he perceives around him: "apple trees" blossoming, "big-boned slavic girls, rich / in marrow, on their way to work," and the dominant feature of the scene,

> my neighbor boy with a football
> calling his dog in the heaven
> of his own back yard.

Welch calls upon Bryant to "look down," and, by implication, bless this scene of innocent bliss with the football flying "over the / sensual mouths of the poppies." And he calls again, "Bear Bryant, look down," reminding the coach that

> once again it's spring practice time
> and the leaves of the dandelions

II. "End-Zones Scored with Darkness"

are speaking longer and longer vowels.
[*Arete* 2.1, 30]

With its evocation of spring, its parallel between Bryant and Williams, and the suggestion that the ideas the dandelions are on the verge of articulating fall within the realm of the "things" the deceased coach concerned himself with in this world, Welch's poem is an anomaly among the portraits of coaches done by poets. My final example of this type is also unique in having been written by a football coach, Mike Rainnie, whom I mentioned above. A little rough around the edges, "Line Coach" records the confession of a high school coach who has spent his professional life turning innocent boys into football players. He documents the "broken limbs" he has seen, the "bones piercing skin," the eyes that "swim in blood." But even with his knowledge of the price the game exacts, he "keeps sending them back." Ultimately the cumulative vision of pain takes its psychological toll on the speaker. While the young men who have emerged each year stride "to their last game of the year" on Thanksgiving morning, their "Steel eyes flashing behind frozen / breath," they are blind in their pride and optimism to what the coach sees: "The carcass ... making drag marks / In the morning frost behind them" (*Aethlon* 8.1, 192).

Rainnie's unsettling vision of mortality is a far cry from Clifford Hill's coaching philosophy and it represents the degree to which the two other outstanding features of football poems (the emphasis on practice as much as games and the ubiquity of Death) are bound up in poems having to do with coaches. The inordinate amount of attention given to practices in football poems suggests that the essence of the game, at least in the memories of those who write about it, resides in the work and pain, the drills, along with the endurance and frequent humiliation they create. In the minds of the poets, as many victories and defeats are suffered on the practice field as in the stadium.

In the poetry of no other sport does practice figure so prominently, if it is a factor at all. Dennis Trudell's "The Jump Shooter" describes a man practicing his jump shot in an impromptu shooting match with a stranger on a shadowy urban playground, but there are no drills and there is no coach present. Numerous baseball poems offer fathers and sons or fathers and daughters working on hitting or pitching, but the emphasis in all of these is on the relationship forged and not the exercise itself. Only football poets such as Gildner in "First Practice," Dickey in "The Bee," and Smith in "Head Feint…" look back on the wind sprints and humiliating one-on-one blocking drills, and highlight the genuine drudgery of practice. Brett Ralph in "Practice Field" remembers getting hit and having it hurt more than usual, especially when the scrapes and cuts incurred in practice would be re-injured every day, never fully healing until the season was finally over. Ralph's speaker is a young jogger, a former player who has left organized football after eleven years of playing at every available level, including a year in intercollegiate competition. He abandoned football despite his father's admonition that he would be a *"quitter"* (*Aethlon* 7.1, 130) his whole life. He pauses to watch a practice when a ball is thrown his way. He pauses to watch a practice when a ball is thrown his way. He picks it up, and tosses it back into the field. Despite his admitting that practices energizes him, he resists the urge to reenter the fray and ignores his former teammate's inquiry as to why that *"big guy"* isn't out there, and fulfills his father's prediction by quite literally running away. "I keep running" (192), he says in the poem's last line.

It is wholly consistent with the pattern already established that in more than fifty lines Ralph's jogger never once refers to having played in a game. His only direct references to his life in football are to practice. Practice and the lessons derived from it are also what remain in the mind of William Greenway's speaker in "Spider Drill." Here the memory of a one-on-one confrontation between himself and a boy named Joe, "the / biggest and meanest in the third / grade," torments the speaker. The speaker won the initial confrontation, carrying the ball across a circle of dirt through his opponent, swelling with pride when he handed the ball to the coach on the other side. But Joe was only momentarily vanquished, coming back on the other boy from his blind side, knocking him down in the dust at the coach's feet. The coach praised Joe, and admonished the one on the ground: "Don't you *never* quit" (*Arete* 3.2, 36)

As an adult, having internalized the coach's message, he replays the drill over and over in his mind, not hating Joe, but actually taking Joe's part, urging him to "blindside the kid / in the red pants, / kick him / when he's down," so that he will always remember what he learned that day, that

there's only one
emotion, huge, sitting in the center, all
the deadly sins and virtues, shame
and love, hate and pride, patience,
greed and envy, even revenge just legs.
                                                    [36]

The poet's point is not merely that the experience taught the boy a lesson (that much is clear), but that the lesson is reductive, deriving from such harsh conditions and under the tutelage of such a sadistic mentor.

Finally, it should come as no surprise that Death is a persistent presence in any sports poem. Defeat is an intrinsic factor in sporting contests and all defeats are microcosmic deaths. Moreover, the process of aging, which is most dramatic in endeavors dependent on the body, is quite literally a natural and constant reminder of the athlete's mortality. But while Death haunts the margins of most sports poems, its presence in football poetry is overwhelming. Football has such a strong connection with Death that Brooke Horvath, when contemplating a doctor's cancer diagnosis in "Weathering March: Thoughts While Driving," thinks of football and autumn weather, even though it is spring. In Larry Rubin's "Saturday Afternoon" football traffic headed for the game becomes entangled with a funeral procession creating the possibility of funeral goers finding "themselves in bleacher seats" (*Lanced*, 31), and the spectators being mistaken for mourners as they leave the stadium on their way home. Randall Jarrell in "Say Goodbye to Big Daddy" identifies Death as Lipscomb's final opponent.

Death looms over more than a dozen works, sometimes as a probable result of the pain and injury a player might inflict on his opponent as in Dickey's "In the Pocket," where his NFL quarterback, his protection breaking down, strives to hit his receiver downfield in enemy territory. He must deliver his pass "before death and the ground" embrace him. He must "LEAP STAND KILL DIE STRIKE / Now" (*Eyebeaters*, 36). David Allan Evans evokes a similar feeling in "Watching Tackles in Slow Motion," in which the predatory tackle is compared to a shark, a hawk, or a polar bear

come from a death
in the jawed and frozen green

saying
I will always find you always find you.
[*Train Windows*, 27]

   Still other poems are elegies to young men: Jim Connolly's # 10 whose drowning is described in "Home Movies," Darrell Stafford's Travis Cox from "Travis Cox Dies on a Light Pole," or Nancy Viera Couto's "football / hero" ("Equestrians," *The Face in the Water*, 3) who died when a train hit his car. None of these characters is described as having been injured in football, but they all seem to have been somehow doomed because of their association with it. Elegies for older men include Dickey's poem for Lombardi, Jarrell's for "Big Daddy," or Ed Hirsch's tribute to his dead high school coach, "Execution." Like Dickey's Lombardi, Hirsch's coach was obsessed with winning. He drove his charges hard, stressing execution above all else, blocking and tackling fundamentals which, when mastered, would lead to each play's perfection, but his players never realized his ideal. Their adolescent awkwardness always overshadowed the meticulous planning. Recalling his last encounter with the coach, Hirsch describes the "cancer stencilled into his face" (*The Night Parade*, 39) how "he looked wobbly and stunned by illness" (39). The spectral presence sends Hirsch back to a game in his senior year against a disciplined and methodical downstate team that not only beat them, they

> battered us all afternoon
> With a vengeance, ... destroyed us with timing
> And power, with deadly, impersonal authority.
> Machine-like fury, perfect execution.
>
> [40]

The poem's final, compelling word, stitching together the coach's favorite concept, defeat, and death, brings home to Hirsch the fact that no matter how much one practices and inveighs against losing, there will always be someone or something more skilled, disciplined, or powerful that you cannot defeat. The only team that executes perfectly is the one that might be represented exclusively by the chalked zeroes the coach drew on the blackboard for "skull sessions."
   Dave Smith makes strong use of the nihilism represented by these

zeroes in one of the most chilling indictments of football's violence, "Running Back." "Much of what is seen is best avoided" (*In the House of the Judge*, 30), he says in the first line. He goes on to record what might better be avoided: the "lips squeezed grape- like," his "own teeth" littering the turf, coaches who "see the field sideways," and tell their players: "*This is a football, / you don't have no idea but it!*" (30). The running back himself survives by not seeing clearly. Repeatedly the poet makes reference to squinting, to going "slant," to seeing "badly" the "blurred chalk" which represents the coach's assessment of the game just played. The reality of the game is so brutal that when he encounters the face of an opponent above the "line of butts" formed by his blockers, the running back converts it, along with his blockers, into an abstraction. He tries to run "artfully ... direct, disguised, at the zero's middle." He ends saying, "I don't have to look for what will be / there, dark, pure, calling incomprehensibly" (31). "Running Back" is the thinking person's football poem, an existentialist's nightmare that goes beyond death to the great dark void.

It is instructive at this point to compare "Running Back" with the self-reflexive poems examined in the previous chapter. Smith's poem, with its emphasis on indirection, on looking at the world aslant and out of focus, bears certain similarities to Robert Francis's "Pitcher." Francis also stresses obliqueness and eccentricity. But the pitcher's goal, according to Francis, is ultimately to communicate. It's just that the batter will understand that communication too late to do anything about it. It's no accident that the rhetorical tools which facilitate a unique kind of understanding in "Pitcher" become in the football poem squinting and indirection, strategies of avoidance. The running back knows without looking directly what will be on the other side of the scrimmage line, calling out "incomprehensively." Francis's pitcher is a poet. Smith's running back is a doomed animal on the brink of the abyss whose "artful" running is not "poetry in motion," but numbing, destructive repetition.

My final example of a poem which equates football with Death is Rodney Jones's "Sweep." Visiting his family home in the rural South, the speaker accompanies his father to a local garage where the mechanics want to talk only "of high school / and who has died from each class" (*The Unborn*, 19). He has spent the three days since returning home "listening to an obituary," he writes, and while the father and one of the mechanics "trade the names of the dead," his own former teammates on the gridiron, he thinks "of football" and how life here in this small town is mostly waiting for death. While the others talk, he sees himself, in a vision similar to that experienced while Richard Jackson's center fielder is waiting for the fly ball to drop in "Center Field." He is

> dropping back deep in the secondary
> under the chill and pipe smoke of a canceled October
> while the sweep rolls toward me from the line of scrimmage.

He watches teammates in front of him crumble under the onslaught, people who have died in real life, "cut down,"

> and I'm shifting on the balls of my feet,
> bobbing and saving one nearly hopeless feint,
> one last plunge for the blockers
> and the ballcarrier who follows the sweep,
> and it comes, and comes on.
>
> [19]

The sweep, the thing itself, not just a consequence of the game or its by-product, is equated here with Death.

Obviously, one can account for the emphasis on death in these poems as a natural extension of the very real fear of injury or the memories of injuries, scars both physical and psychic which the experience of football makes almost inevitable. Perhaps the game's autumnal setting evokes cultural memories of harvest festivals and their ritual sacrifice of the corn king to insure the continuity of the crops. Only in Neal Bowers's "Losing Season" does the possibility seem to exist for a redemptive potential in this sacrifice; however, redemption even here is more apparent than real.

In his own ode to autumn, Bowers records nature's failure to maintain its vitality through the winter. Trees "have failed / in their experiment / to become solid green." Flowers have "given up." In the midst of what Bowers describes as "losing and letting go," flies "turn dark as frozen meat / and stick to the windows" (*Arete* 3.2, 141). But just as Keats's "barred clouds bloom the soft-dying day" in the third stanza of his ode, Bowers enlivens his bleak landscape with sounds from the high school stadium, where the home team's chant

blooms on the frosted air
and floats across the fields,
a hope made visible:
"Next year, next year, next year."

[141]

The term "chant" deepens the scene's ritualistic potential, but the broad seasonal vision the poet establishes in his first two stanzas more than offsets the limited perspective the fans express. Despite the success of any team in a given year, autumn will always be a losing season.

Similarly, Michael Bettencourt's "The Freshman Football Game" records the fumbling performance of two freshman squads in an almost empty stadium. In the first stanza the poem seems to be an account of semi-comic ineptitude. The players stumble around the field. Their equipment is too big. They are, after all, children. As the rookies untangle themselves from a pile-up late in a game, no one notices the signs of impending winter, the foreshadowing of the seasonal death in the offing. All attempt as well to shrug off the minor injuries the players sustain, harbingers of more serious damage the young men might suffer should they continue playing football.

Quite appropriately, given general tendencies in most football literature, Bettencourt remarks that after the game ends, the grounds crew "strips the field of memory" (*Arete* 4.2, 98), since what we cannot remember we are doomed to repeat. The lights go out, then the last vestiges of autumn hunker down along the field between "end-zones scored with darkness" (98). The poem ends. The game ends. Lights go out. The evening comes to a close. The season rapidly wears on toward winter. As Frost says in another autumn poem, "Essence of winter sleep is on the night," and the same questions that will trouble the "human sleep" ("After Apple Picking," *The Poetry of Robert Frost*, 68) of Frost's apple-picker should weigh upon Bettencourt's players, coaches, spectators, and the readers of his poem. The term "end-zones" carries the definitive sense of closure here, and suggests that the promise embodied by these *fresh*men is also doomed since their end-zones, and, in the poets' eyes at least, those of any of the rest of us who play football, are "scored with darkness."

Messenger argues persuasively that the nature of football, with its violence, anonymity and fierce restrictiveness, combined with late autumn's eschatological overtones, demand that the writer of football fiction look outside of the game itself for the expression of creative values. Even in its most positive manifestation the game represents non-growth. It is, according to Messenger, "structurally de-individualizing," making "the battle ... so very strong in football for individual self definition" (261). With some qualification, the same assessment of football emerges from an examination of the poetry. If anything, the concentration and unity required in the poems (there is little time for the poet to develop relationships, other careers, subplots) make for an even bleaker scenario than in the prose.

The poets' vision of football is overwhelmingly negative, unalloyed by the moments of grace and beauty or opportunities for transcendence that arise in poems about other sports, especially baseball. Absent too from these poems is baseball's emphasis on language, perhaps because communication on the field tends to be clipped, exact, and severely curtailed by helmets with face masks. The sidelines, awash in crowd noise, band music, and the racket of substitutions shuttling in and out allow little of the casual conversation afforded by the baseball dugout. In the locker room language either manifests itself in celebratory whoops and shouts or, for the losers, is simply non-existent. Even the creation of admonitory myths seems discouraged in football because creation itself is smothered by work, injury and death.

When, for example, Peter Meinke pays tribute to James Dickey in "To an Athlete Turned Poet," he describes a man who once lived for contact, the "weekend hero" who throve on "cracking" (*Trying to Surprise God*, 69) but who is now gone soft. In place of the scrimmage line he now crosses "line after line" of poems, his "heart red- / dogging with rage and joy over the broken backs / of words words words." Meinke seems to take Dave Smith's caveat that "words are the poet's enemies" at face value, without taking into account Smith's qualification that they are also his "conspirators, and only allies" (*Local Assays,* 29). Undermining the power that Meinke says Dickey transferred from the gridiron to the page is the destructive language which controls the "creative" process. Apparently, Meinke envisions Dickey's having transferred the *agon* of football to the field of writing, a notion that further distinguishes the football poet from his baseball counterpart who, more often than not, *plays* with language. Even when football poets *want* to channel the game's energy to creative ends, the game itself defeats them.

Football poems are like terse underground messages smuggled from prison camps back to our homes and families. Football, like war, compels us to purge our minds of the brutality we have suffered as well as inflicted on others, so that we might convince our sons, whom we entrust to demonic surrogates, to re-enact our sacrifice. The grim reaper takes his place as the 12th man in virtually every huddle, and, to paraphrase James Dickey, it's a wonder any of us survive football.

III

Courtly Love, or the Sound of One Hand Shooting

The Basketball Poem

Poems about baseball and football reveal consistent motifs which define each game and accentuate what we as individuals and as a culture derive from them. Baseball, "the poet's game," is recreated through the gauzy eye of nostalgia, defined and preserved through language, and is often the source of our identities. Football poems, on the other hand, stress sacrifice and labor, humiliation and injury as often as not at the hands of one's own teammates, and the demonic father figure to whom we entrust our physical and spiritual well-being — the coach. Baseball poetry thrives on the misty diamonds of childhood, football on the cleat-harrowed fields of adolescence. Basketball, the youngest of the three major sports in the United States, inspires poems of young adulthood through middle age set mostly in playgrounds, schoolyards and after-hours recreation centers.

The time frame for most basketball poems is the present, although a persistent minority voice creates in some of these poems a nostalgic fantasy that locates the soul of the game in an almost mythical rural Heartland, hoopland's "field of dreams." Thus Dennis Trudell in "The Years" views from a passing train a kid's jump shot rising

> toward a bright new basketball net
> above gravel between house and barn
> [*Aethlon* 11.2, 130]

and connects his future, at age fifty, to the success of the shot, although a grain elevator blocks his view before the outcome of the shot can be determined. The poem's title clearly suggests Trudell is viewing his own beginnings from the train window and that he sees in the boy's shot the opportunity for his own resurrection. In "The Touch" Justin Mitcham thanks his mother for demonstrating "what a softer touch could do" (*Somewhere in Ecclesiastes*, 5) when she left her work in the kitchen to step out into the driveway and show him her set shot. In a similar vein, Aleda Shirley in "A Basketball Game at Newburgh Middle School" projects a vision of one of the young cheerleaders several years in the future, standing on "a porch in light snow" (*Rilke's Children*, 10) watching her son in the driveway shooting free throws and thinking back to a moment when all eyes were on her in the school gym. In "Crisis on Toast," as Sherman Alexie and his father drive around the reservation, they watch two boys playing hoops and are drawn into the game in an effort to recapture (or revise) their past. While individually these works are devoid of racial overtones, they suggest in the aggregate a yearning for origins which lie outside of the urban game.

Finally, basketball poems celebrate the creation of ephemeral identities dependent upon the ebb and flow of a particular competition and the degree to which the individual manages to lose himself and get "into" his game. Poem after poem stresses getting into "the zone," rising above physical or sociological limitations—transcendence.

Since basketball, more than baseball or football, relies upon quickness, speed, and jumping ability, and, as any athlete knows, the legs always go first, one would expect a good deal of emphasis in basketball poems on loss. Indeed, loss dominates many of these poems, and its effects are more obvious in basketball than in most other sports not only because of the rigors of the game, but also because of its "being so physically close to the worlds around it" (*Full Court*, 9). The lost step, missed pass, or fumbled rebound is there for the world to see. Despite the potential for transforming this sense of loss into despair or self-pity, writers of basketball poems tend to focus upon what remains rather than what has vanished or worn away, either by simply resolving to accept their diminished abilities or celebrating idealized versions of themselves which are enhanced by basketball's potential for intimacy. Only baseball poems offer more parent/son relationships than basketball poems, and, surprisingly, many of the basketball poems feature mothers. But mostly the intimacy develops among groups of men who play together so regularly, as Robert Hamblin acknowledges, "only lovers read [their] moves as well" as they do each other's ("Half-Court Advantage," *Aethlon* 5.1, 179).

In emphasizing venue and transcendence, basketball poetry parallels such basketball fiction as David Shields's *Heroes*, Todd Walton's *Inside Moves*, and Jay Neugeboren's *Big Man*. In one significant respect, however, the poems depart from the fiction — the dearth of poetry dedicated to the so-called "black game." Virtually every critic who has analyzed the game since the early 1970s has emphasized the degree to which black players have shaped basketball. Jeremy Larner in *Drive, He Said* (1964) identified two contrasting styles in the game, but asserted that "the white boss grimly prevails over the Negro," and that the black style is "more joyful to watch or play, ... but it is the white boss style that wins" (110–111). How things changed in the last quarter of the twentieth century! Both Michael Novak and Michael Oriard, reacting to a more contemporary game, stress the analogy between the black game and jazz, and Messenger argues that "basketball is the first major American sport to be redefined in its standards of play, its folk culture, its mores, and its language by a specific subculture with basketball's resultant dislocation in the white psyche and overemphasis in the black psyche" (395).

Black dominance in both the style and substance of the game is undeniable, yet only about one-tenth of the roughly one hundred poems I have examined for this chapter even mention black athletes. There are relatively straightforward tributes to black athletes in Diane Ackerman's "Patrick Ewing Takes a Foul Shot," William Matthews's "In Memory of the Utah Stars" (almost totally focused on Moses Malone), and two poems by Tom Meschery — "As It Should Be" and "To Wilt Chamberlain" (the latter well-meaning but dangerously close to racist in describing Chamberlain as "Tropical and dense / As the jungle" of his ancestors (*Over the Rim*, 40). Other poems try to capture the speed and improvisational panache of the "black game" and contrast it with "white man's basketball" in traditional language. "Charge" by Christopher Gilbert, "Makin' Jump Shots" by Michael S. Harper, and "Slam, Dunk, and Hook" by Yusef Komunyakaa fall into this category.[1] Finally, there are poems that employ the language and rhythms of the inner city playground to portray mimetically the essence of the game as jazz and the men who play it as consummate artists. Two poems by Quincy Troupe, "A Poem for 'Magic'" and "Forty-one Seconds on a Sunday in June, in Salt Lake City, Utah," and a piece by Tim Seibles entitled "For Brothers Everywhere," best represent this approach.

Christopher Gilbert's "Charge" fully captures the individual competitiveness of the schoolyard, and the opportunity for players to momentarily transcend racial, sociological and economic limitations through performance. Four times in "Charge's" twenty-six lines, Willie, Gilbert's focal character in the poem, whom he describes as "Gwen Brooks' player from the streets" (*Across the Mutual Landscape*," 59) says, with minor variations, "*Gimme the ball*," trying to keep his two-man team alive through his own heroics, since only the winners keep playing, and Willie "plays like his being is at stake." His moves represent his life, Gilbert argues, and his goal is "the rapture gained with presence." Willie's "rapture," a mystical breakthrough, elevates him above his human opponents, and takes on more profound implications when Gilbert identifies Willie's real opponents as "Death and Uniformity." Thus, when Willie pleads, "*Gimme the ball ... Gimme the goddamn ball*," (59) his goal is not merely victory in the game but transcendence of the human condition.

In his introduction to *Full Court: Stories and Poems for Hoop Fans*, Dennis Trudell points out that within the confined area of a basketball court "the yearning is always for empty space"(9). Given the dimensions of the court and the fact that it is filled with other bodies, that empty space is most available above the crowd. In achieving transcendence, one rises into space that is not available to anyone else. In his tribute to "Magic" Johnson, for example, Quincy Troupe says that the professional star created his "own space" (*Skulls Along the River*, 111). Troupe's poem builds through a series of coordinate phrases, first verbs, "juked and shook," then verbs used as adjectives, "shake and bake," then back to verbs, "shake and glide," the variations on "shake" infusing the language with a shimmering quality, the language accumulating without punctuation to the inevitable conclusion that Johnson is indeed "magic," a "shonuff shaman man" (111).

The language and style of "A Poem for 'Magic'" expand its scope beyond the professional arena to the black community at large. Johnson is a heroic role model who has shrugged off the historical chains of oppression through athletics. Tim Seibles goes a step further than Troupe's implicit message, however, in "For Brothers Everywhere," a description of schoolyard basketball that portrays neighborhood young men achieving their own kind of escape. While Seibles uses language almost identical to Troupe's, his imagery is even more transcendent, a significant difference, given the fact that these are "ordinary" young men in a neighborhood venue, not professional stars with multi-million-dollar contracts. The baskets are "pinned / like thunderclouds to the sky's wide chest." The "brothers" are "palming the sun and throwing it down." They play "beyond / summer, beyond weather, beyond / everything that moves," and they pull up "from the edge of the world, hangin' like air itself hangs in air, / an' gravidy gotta giv'em up" (*Hurdy Gurdy*, 12). Mimicking the improvisational flow of the schoolyard game, "For Brothers..." flows in one long sentence, and its only explicit reference to deprivation or discrimination appears in the assertion that the young men play beyond sunset, "without even / a crumb of light from the city," yet Seibles's targeted audience, coupled with his repeated emphasis on escape ("gravidy" is social and economic as well as physical), mark this poem as a more resonant black anthem than Troupe's.

Achieving transcendence and exploring its consequences preoccupies most of the poets who write about basketball, who make few distinctions between black or white players, urban playgrounds or small-town schoolyards, country rock music or jazz (or what might be a more appropriate metaphor for contemporary black basketball, improvisational rap). But Messenger, who argues that in fiction both black and white players play for transcendence, makes a distinction between the white player's mystical experience and the black player's cultural event. The distinction lies in the black player's victory over his immediate surroundings, his personal past, and the burdens of racial history, as well as the limitations of physical laws and mortality that the white player must overcome.

Interestingly enough, the basketball poems of Sherman Alexie, a Native American, take him back to the poverty, alcoholism and domestic dysfunction of the reservation, even though, as he says in "Native Hero," he can "never call the reservation home" (*Aethlon* 6.1, 146). Through basketball Alexie forges a curious love/hate relationship with his past. In "Crisis on Toast" he and his father drive through the reservation, the father regaling the son with old stories about drinking, when they come upon two boys shooting basketball on a farm lot. The father, aging and overweight from too much beer, tells his son that he had played ball like these two slender boys in his youth. As they exit their car, heading for a pickup game with the two farm boys, the poet, fearful that his father might embarrass himself or even have a heart attack, says, "I've never been more afraid / of the fear in any man's eyes" (*Full Court*, 324). Like Seymour Reuben, the "native hero" who scores 68 points in a game and seems ageless, the father is tied to his past. Basketball is, ironically, an anchor, not a vehicle for escape, literally or figuratively.

Flick Webb, John Updike's "Ex-basketball Player," is also tethered to his past. Updike's piece is an anomaly among basketball poems, but a work firmly centered in the mainstream of sports poems in general. It portrays the classic "washed-up jock" whose archetype appears in Homer's Nestor, who wishes he "were young again and the strength still unshaken within me" (*Iliad*, Bk. 23, l. 629, Lattimore trans.) as he was in earlier days when no one was his peer. Flick Webb was purely an institutional player, a scholastic hero who still holds a country record, long after he has apparently given up the game. Now, rather than playing pick-up games in the schoolyard, Flick, an employee of Berth's Garage, substitutes an inner tube for the basketball and dribbles for the amusement of those fans who remember what he was. In his young adulthood, a time cherished by most basketball poets, he has given up the game to spend his off hours at Mae's Luncheonette. Given the time frame of Flick's athletic career, the late '40s, he would, of necessity, have played "white" basketball, but two small details in Updike's portrait of Flick look forward to the kind of game and the kind of player extolled by contemporary poets. Updike's narrator (a critical feature of this poem often overlooked by readers) remarks that "the ball loved Flick" (*Collected Poems*, 4), and that his "hands were like wild birds," two qualities which undoubtedly contributed to Flick's heroics, separated him from the controlled exercise now labeled "white" basketball, and, in their emphasis upon the ball's affinity for his hands and his own *natural* touch, established him as a precursor of the contemporary basketball player. The goal of the fictional basketball player, according to Messenger, is to achieve "transcendence in which the player becomes 'at one' with the goal and rim, the goal becoming that of a touch that results in no touch with the rim…" (388). Perhaps Flick was a has-been because he was ahead of his time.

Unlike Flick, most former high school basketball players depicted in contemporary poems keep at the game. Although they might have lacked Flick's notoriety and touch even as young men, they continue to run the boards and pursue "the zone," and when finesse proves irretrievable, they take what they can get. David Hilton's "I Try to Turn in My Jock" (alternatively entitled "The Poet Tries to Turn in His Jock") serves as a model for poems dealing with this subject. After faking out a younger player, and getting open for a shot at the top of the key, Hilton's alter ego sustains a serious ankle injury which triggers an inner debate through which he quickly considers alternatives to being an easy mark for younger players on weekends. He thinks of joining the Y, working out and enjoying martinis afterward. But the argument ends abruptly when he looks up and sees the successful result of his shot. Hilton's poem ends with a coda any over-the-hill athlete can use as a rationale for continuing to compete. He may be slowing down, prone to injury, not as flexible as in his prime,

> But shit,
> The shot goes in.
> [*Huladance*, 58]

Other versions of Hilton's declaration range from a resonant echo in Bobby Byrd's "One of the Meanings of the 1987 NBA Championship Series" to softened, somewhat idealized accounts of regular games among peers in which the courts are halved and expectations are lowered. The critical issues in theses poems are the regular competition and the camaraderie it fosters. Byrd's response to questions of the ultimate meaning, and "most of all — death" that arise as he and his aging friends are "pushing the ball / and ourselves, up / and down a short court" is: "Fuck it. / We are friends" (*Aethlon* 5.2, 130). Robert Gibb and his friends "surrender / To the old rhythms of play" in "Night Basketball" and seek to bring "that something in us / Which wants to rise … into play / Once more" (*Arete* 3.2, 58). Boyd White, who is even at twenty-two "too slow" and out of shape, goes up strong, "Hoping the shot's good / And that I never come down" ("Low Post," *Aethlon* 7.1, 121).

In no poem is the resolve to accept what remains better expressed than in Robert Hamblin's "Half-Court Advantage." The players' familiarity with the half-court game provides a little edge in their thrice-weekly games against mostly younger opponents, that and the fact that they know each other's moves and tendencies so well. They even win occasionally. They all realize, however, that

> What matters in this remaining space,
> where all contests are played close
> to the ground, is the sound and rhythm
> of ball on pavement, the flow
> of the moment, press of flesh on flesh

that allows them to "learn again the strategy of survival," to "practice the art of staying alive" (*Aethlon* 5.1, 180).

In Mark DeFoe's "Hoop League" players who have lost their youthful skills can only look back at their heroics in high school. Yet some "hands recall that last caress, / the wrist snap, the fingers' sweet goodbye" of the shot that won the championship (*Arete* 3.2, 91). Now, competing before empty bleachers, some of these players retain that early vision and still "play to find the rightness, the rhythm, zone," that "other element" where they discover "nothing but net," and can "in-your-face the world." Ultimately, their dream, like that of Chris Gilbert's Willie, is to hang "windmilling over mortal earth — / suspended forever, lightning / flashing in the slam-dunk's thunder" (*Across*, 59).

Unquestionably, the goal of DeFoe's hoop league players is transcendence, and even though its final instrument is a power play, preparation lies in the muscle memory of the caress and the "fingers' sweet goodby" (59). More important, DeFoe's players are of indeterminate race and socioeconomic background. They could be all-white factory workers, racially mixed college professors, or all-black players from varied professions and backgrounds. The game, however, with its mild "trash talk" and the dream of rising above all mortal bounds is identical to that described by Gilbert in "Charge." The absence of "white boss" basketball even among aging athletes derives not so much from poets' liberal tendencies or vision of racial harmony as from the domination of basketball by blacks to the extent that the only concept of the game which exists for the poet today is the so-called "black game." To write about basketball, especially when such novelistic issues as character development and socio-economic determinism are eliminated, is to write about the black game, at least insofar as an ideal game exists against which all play is measured. Slow, mechanical play and physical awkwardness are not so much "white play" as they are simply "not basketball."

Touch and the ability to play beyond oneself, at one with the ball or "in the zone," are the qualities most esteemed by poets who observe contemporary basketball, although the cause/effect relationship between the two is unclear. Does "touch" lead to play beyond oneself, or does being "in the zone" engender "touch"? As with all mystical experiences, causal explanations are scarce, since the experience by definition is most often *received* rather than *achieved*. Adequate language is also difficult to formulate, since one is describing for the most part what is inexplicable. The early Romantics, for example, until they developed their own language, relied upon orthodox religious terminology to describe their glimpses of the noumenal world. Our poets rely on the language of personal intimacy and affection.

One of Carl Lindner's basketball poems is, in fact, entitled "First Love." In it he describes the intimacy that exists between a young shooter and the ball after countless hours spent shooting baskets in his driveway "court." Points are insignificant, since there is no opponent. The primary goals are style and "feel." The speaker's ball "always ... came back" to him. "I loved ... waiting / for the touch," he says. When he had it, he and the ball worked together. He "could feel / the ball hunger / ing to clear / the lip of the rim." He could sense both himself and the ball, "the two of us / falling through" (*Angling*, 35). In another piece, "When I Got It Right," Lindner further develops the idea of playing outside himself, "in the zone." His ending, in fact, would fit remarkably well in Eugen Herrigel's *Zen and the Art of Archery*. When he had it, Lindner writes, the ball would glide "like a blessing / over the rim," or "kissing off glass" it would fall softly "into the skirt of net." Once the magic had begun, he "couldn't miss." Even as dark fell, the ball, before it left his hand, "was sure" (*Shooting Baskets*, 63).

Similarly, Dennis Trudell's "The Jump Shooter" ends with an overweight, over-thirty-five player dropping shot after shot into the basket as darkness deepens over the playground where he has been joined by the poem's speaker. The speaker, who has wordlessly floated into the game, alternates shots with the first man and is lifted out of a sour mood by watching the stranger in full possession of his "touch."

Trudell's entire poem is suffused with softness: the failing light with its muted colors and shadows, the relative quiet (neither man speaks), and the slow, fluid movements of the players. The poem itself illustrates perfectly the marriage of form and content as its short, three-line stanzas flow into one another with the ease of the shooter's style, the fluidity of the speaker's taking up the game, and his smoothness in ghosting away, uplifted, as the ball hung against the evening sky

> then suddenly filled
> the net
> [*Fragments*, 73]

while he walked away, transformed by the magic he has momentarily shared.

Michael McFee's "Shooting Baskets at Dusk" echoes the tone of "The Jump Shooter" and Lindner's "First Love." All three poems take place at dusk. In each situation the shooter experiences a kind of magic. Like Lindner, McFee eliminates even the hint of competition, featuring a solitary player much like the baseball pitcher in William Matthews's "The Hummer." But whereas Matthews's speaker engages in "fierce moral work," calling his own balls and strikes, striving to strike out the batters and simultaneously "hit" the tennis ball thrown at the garage door, Lindner's and McFee's basketball players float almost effortlessly in "the zone." Neither is the "game" they play designated as practice, even though it is an exercise designed to hone the players' skills. These players are simply playing basketball, not sweating out arduous "two-a-days" like football players. McFee's shooter "will never be happier than this," as he becomes "absorbed in the rhythm" of shoot, rebound, dribble, the ball almost magically returning to him after each shot as it bounces off the brick wall behind the basket. McFee, though, takes the blending of Trudell's speaker into the shadows surrounding the court one step further, by having darkness encroach upon the shooter's game as it is still being played. The young man becomes "just a shadow and a sound," still playing, the ball burning "in his vanished hands." Other poets describe players rising above the crowd, playing beyond themselves, hanging at the rim "forever" but McFee's shooter achieves transcendence through such a complete absorption into the game that his corporeality is momentarily jeopardized (*Vanishing Acts*, 9).

In "Foul Shots: A Clinic," William Matthews attempts a more analytical approach to technique, echoing the instructions an aspiring shooter might receive at a coaches' clinic: "Be perpendicular to the basket / toes avid for the line" (*Selected Poems*, 57). But the instruction breaks down as abstract in the context's overwhelming circularity — the ball, the basket, the foul circle, even the round head of a nail in the gym floor, all complicating the issue of perpendicularity. Even though the shooter's body isn't round, it "isn't / perpendicular," Matthews argues, then cites the relative merits of the collarbone as a reference point. From then on, however, Matthews warns that the guidelines become spiritual. In what might again be a page from Herrigel, the shooter must simultaneously relax and concentrate, must "aim / for the front of the rim but miss it / deliberately." He must shoot 200 shots a day but train himself never to be bored.

Matthews's final twelve lines attest to the power of love as the informing principle necessary for attaining perfection. "You have to love" to practice, he says. "You'd love to be good" at shooting, but it's not a love so powerful that it would motivate you to "shoot 200 foul shots / every day." In fact, the speaker claims that those "lovingly unlaunched" free throws that exist only in his and his auditor's minds—since neither possesses the love that would lead him to really practice —

> circle eccentrically
> in a sky of stolid orbits
> as unlike as you and I are
> from the arcs those foul shots
> leave behind when they go in.
> [57]

By stressing the contrast in the shooters and the shots, Matthews returns to the geometrical problems posed at the beginning of the poem. That paradox is resolved by resorting to the spiritual. In effect, Matthews's ending takes refuge in the spiritual as well, or at least the imagination. Since both he and his "pupil" lack the love necessary to achieve the ease which comes with drudgery, foul shot satori, they reach perfection in their minds. Matthews's emphasis on love rather than desire or ambition as the spirit mover in gaining that perfection suggests that today's game, whether one calls it the black game, the natural game, or the zen game, demands the heart's commitment rather than the head's or the gut's.

Kent Cartwright attempts to capture what Novak terms "the blurred and intricate designs woven by the paths through which all five [players] cast a spell upon the opposition" (*The Joy of Sports*, 100) in "Scoring." Cartwright's controlling metaphor in the beginning of the poem is electrical. A pass "zaps ... like a mad electron," for example. The game he describes resembles as much as anything a video game. The pace is furious. A player "fuses in circuit / to the weird ganglion of bobbing rubber ... head fakes, / and breaks, slicing the stunned circle, a dazzling filament..." (*Arete* 1.2, 41). But the language changes at the player's approach to the basket. His touch is "soft as fur," but the shooter is forgotten as all attention shifts to the ball which

> jolts a smudgy kiss
> on the cold, clear glass,
> hangs away on the lip,
> moody, weighing the balance,
> sighs through the net
> like the whisper
> of love.
>
> [41]

The language of intimacy abounds in these poems. One of Tom Meschery's poems is entitled "Basketball: A Love Song Because It Is" (*Over the Rim*, 28). Alexie's Seymour Reuben cradles a basketball with more tenderness than he would have shown to "any baby he may have fathered" ("Native Hero," *Aethlon* 6.1, 146) as he travels from reservation to reservation. Lindner's shot goes "kissing" off the glass through the "skirt of net" ("When I Got It Right"). A hook shot "kisses the rim" to begin Edward Hirsch's "Fast Break" (*Wild Gratitude*, 8). In Kevin Miller's "Talking Back," the ball's "wet side smacks / a moon shaped kiss" (*Aethlon* 11.2, 66) on the backboard. The gestures of B. H. Fairchild's "Old Men Playing Basketball" are "in love / again with the pure geometry of curves" (*Art of the Lathe*, 45). Bob Hamblin emphasizes "the flow / of the moment, press of flesh on flesh" and "togetherness" (not teamwork) in "Half-court Advantage." And in his "Pick and Roll" he describes the ball "cradled in grateful hands and gently, deftly, / guided home to roost" (*Aethlon* 5.1, 179). Kisses, caresses, tender cradling and soft touches are sometimes creative of, sometimes evidence of, being "in the zone." Ironically, as the game has become increasingly physical the language used to describe it has softened, an indication perhaps that the goals of achieving the touch, zoning, transcendence, are not to be forced, but coaxed and courted like a lover.

The game described in these poems is neither white nor black, but in its search for the touch that passeth understanding it inclines toward Zen, which is the central notion of Norman German's "New World in the Morning" which, with perhaps a nod toward James Tate's baseball poem, "The Buddhists Have the Ballfield," features a "Zen Buddhist basketball team" whose players are "at peace with themselves / the fans, the refs," and the "other players." The Buddhists make every shot and politely step aside when the opponent's "star player drives for a layup and, / having nothing to fight for, misses." Sandria Char and Krishna avoid "the karma-disturbing thuds of a dribble," and pass or hand-off the ball down court to Gandhi, waiting "sleepy-eyed under the home town hoop." As might be expected, Gandhi's shot "rises in a perfect silent curve." It doesn't touch the rim but "swishes through the net / like a good soul coming into being." Obviously tongue in cheek, German's poem, which is set in the outskirts of a town in southeast Texas, nevertheless merely exaggerates a trend, which, in the poetry at least, clearly exists. And if words counted on the court, German's closing lines would apply to the All-Star Poets basketball team as well as the Buddhists:

> Tonight they subdue with serenity.
> Next year they take the title.
> [*Worcester Review* 8.2, 68]

IV

Pulling Together

Women's Sports Poems

The photograph of soccer player Brandi Chastain waving her jersey around her head in celebration of the U.S. Women's Soccer Team's victory over China in the 1999 World Cup competition encapsulates in one image the complex and paradoxical nature of women's sports in our culture. On the one hand, the image records not just the stunning victory in the match itself, but also a monumental step of women's athletics toward equality with men's. In stripping off her outer jersey, Chastain, in effect, proclaimed, "We are women. We're the best, and we deserve your respect and admiration." Paradoxes arise, on the other hand, when one recognizes that Chastain's spontaneous demonstration mimicked the celebratory gestures of her male counterparts, thus signifying her implicit endorsement of phallocentric attitudes toward competition and winning. Seen from the perspective of Susan Birrell and Nancy Theberg, the actions of Chastain and her teammates were "resistant" without being "transformative." Through their physical skills and determination they overcame the myriad social barriers impeding the success of female athletes in our culture, yet even in victory they accepted "the structure of relations of power and the ideologies that hold those structures in place" (*Women and Sport*, 363).[1]

Chastain's "resistance" derived in part from the team's victory, but it manifested itself most significantly in her symbolically baring her breasts, historically the most obvious physical "impediment" to women's participation in vigorous physical activity. Unlike the real or fictional athletes subjected to the humiliation of binding or otherwise restricting their breasts in order to compete on the court or field, Chastain unbound them on national television. Ironically, however, the notoriety she gained from her action led to almost instant commodification. Like so many male athletes, she became an image to be bought and sold.

On the soccer field, Chastain triumphed in what Susan J. Bandy in "The Female Athlete as Protagonist" has defined as

> a physical contest, one that requires mastery and demonstration of superior skills in competition against, rather than with another. It has developed in such a way as to demand, value, and reward so-termed masculine qualities such as physicality, aggression, domination, and competition. As such, it has been considered antithetical to the socially-sanctioned and accepted views of femininity which demand compliance, cooperation, and subservience... [83].

Traditional sport, then, "affirms what she [the female athlete] is not, a male. Sport can therefore not be used as a vehicle to affirm her femininity" (84), unless of course, sport and femininity are redefined, transformed, as Birell and Theberge would have it. As a consequence of these paradoxes and contradictions, women's sport offers a mother lode of opportunity for poets. Unfortunately, some women have merely accepted the idolatrous fan's approach to sport, which underlies so much inferior sports poetry written by men and makes it virtually indistinguishable from that poetry. Others highlight the struggle to overcome obstacles created by a phallocentric and phallogocentric sports establishment, sometimes celebrating victory, sometimes lamenting a defeat. A third category of poets transforms sport to make it a uniquely feminine enterprise. That said, there is an element that informs the best sports poems that rarely appears in the works examined in this chapter. Women challenge male authority, question tradition, yet they only infrequently question the enterprise itself.

A striking parallel exists between women in sport and women in the "poetry game," so that when women who write poems about sports are discussed the two subjects complement and play off one another. In fact, when poet and critic Alicia Ostriker assessed the state of women's poetry in her article "In Mind: The Divided Self in Women's Poetry," much of her analysis was remarkably relevant to women's athletics. Ostriker first established that women poets were rebelling against not only the male domination of American letters, but also against the perceived notion that their efforts somehow required validation by the male establishment. She cited Erica Jong's "Bitter Pills for the Dark Ladies" as a representative expression of women's frustration. Jong complains that if a woman gains the approval of the gatekeepers, "the ultimate praise is always a question of nots," meaning that she can be accepted only if she does not violate the rules which they insist she follow (*Poetics*, 112). According to Ostriker, women's poetry, while it is by no means monolithic, reacts to this condescension by expressing four critical themes, which are

> original, important and organically connected with one another. These are the quest for autonomous self-definition; the intimate treatment of the body; the release of anger; and what I call, for want of a better name, the contact imperative [114].[2]

If women's poetry in general suffered the indignity of having to prove itself to the male establishment, how much more difficult must it be for women to succeed in writing poetry focused on sport, which, despite recent trends, remains the most male-dominated enterprise in our culture. One might expect sports poetry by a woman to succeed in direct relation to the poet's demonstrating that, to paraphrase Jong, "she don't throw like a girl."

Certainly, many women's poems about sport are essentially androgynous. Gender distinctions blur in poems of hero worship and in the rare poem by a woman which waxes nostalgic. Diane Ackerman's "Patrick Ewing Takes a Foul Shot," for example, contains none of the indicators Ostiker cites as gender identifiers. Ewing is described in close, imaginative detail, shaping the basketball as if he were packing a snowball as he prepares to shoot a free throw. While effective, Ackerman's poem is not associated with either gender's point of view. Similarly, Lucille Clifton's "Jackie Robinson" and Susan Hall Herport's "One Deep Dish Beauty of a Right" are tributes to Robinson and Jersey Joe Walcott, respectively.[3] Other than the poets' names attached to the work, neither contains a gender signifier, although it might be argued that racial pride supersedes gender issues in both works. A "projected nostalgia" dominates Aleda Shirley's "A Basketball Game at Newburgh Middle School," and Joan Newman's "Rounders" is almost pure nostalgia. Newman recreates a family evening of play on a farm, the kind of domestic scene Brooke Horvath and Sharon Carson cite as one of women's most important contributions to sports poetry. The details of "new hay," a "warm smell on dusk dew," and the fragrance of night flowers provide a backdrop for an uncle, the bowler, who ran out of the darkness, appearing at first to be a fierce competitor, ready to blow the ball by her, but who in the end floated the ball in to her "astounded, waiting bat" (*Poetry,* Oct.-Nov. 1995, 86). The tone and setting remind one of Neal Bowers's "Late Innings," when

> In the west, the sky flares its dull embers,
> grows luminous beyond the horizon as if the lights
> in a distant stadium had been switched on,
> and the last boy digs in at home with the crickets,
> the gathering dew, waiting for the long dark curve.
> [*Helicon Nine* 19, 45]

Other poems lean toward androgyny by exploring a moment, reveling in an experience, or stressing universality. These three categories coalesce in varied proportions in Barbara Smith's "In Balance," Jeanne Lebow's "Running," and Maxine Kumin's "Cross-Country Skiing." Smith observes that transitional moment before anyone has stepped on the dew-covered golf course in the early morning. Clearly more is at stake here, since Smith knows that "offerings and entrances," the first footprints of the day on the course (*Aethlon* 5.1, 72), create symmetry. The reader cannot ignore what remains unsaid in the poem but which is nonetheless required, a counterweight for the early morning optimism — the end of something, failure, loss. Jeanne Lebow's "Running" revels in the physical exuberance of vigorous exercise, with steam rising from the runner's skin as her "thighs push through rain forests" (*Arete* 1.2, 84). Lebow, too, achieves a kind of balance, although it is wholly centered in the moment at which everything flows but is "still." She "drinks" in her surroundings and envisions herself as a "floating center" (94). While Lebow's words are unique, the experience of having broken through, of feeling totally energized, would be understood by anyone who has achieved it. Finally, Kumin's skiing poem, a sonnet which records a stolen moment under the limbs of "hemlocks heavily snowed upon," eschews gender issues for a broader humanitarian/political observation. From her haven the skiier thinks of the "grainy videos of refugees" and contemplates their suffering from her insular quiet under the hemlocks (*Connecting*, 33).

An entire class of poems by women, going back to Marianne Moore's widely anthologized baseball pieces, seeks to convey the insider's knowledge of whatever game is being portrayed. Mostly, these are spectator poems, but I would not characterize their point of view as that of an "outsider, the passive spectator," who, according to Anne Darden, "makes the action on the field meaningful simply by understanding what she is observing" (*Aethlon* 15.1, 4). Although "The Players" by Kim Roberts, in which the observers are "women on bleachers / here to cheer for our men" (*Aethlon* 6.2, 176), clearly delineates the "outsider" as Darden describes her, many other spectator poems unfold from the perspective of the aficionado, who understands the game, its players, the history, and nuances of language. Terence J. Roberts points out that few of us are passive spectators. He writes:

> Even when we see sports actions first hand we do not in some two stage process first see actions in their naked form, as they are-in-themselves, and then remake them through composition, decomposition, or any of the other processes or worldmaking. Rather the seeing is the making and the making is the composing, decomposing, weighting, and so on. And from there we remake and remake again ["The Making and Remaking...," 23].

Thus, the poet, who is first knowledgeable about the game, shapes and reshapes her perceptions in the light of her insights. Gail Mazur's "Baseball" is a case in point. While denying that baseball is a metaphor for life, the poem reveals a knowledge of the game and its fans which would be incomprehensible to an outsider. Mazur's description of "the Kid," who "leaps into the air to catch a ball / that should have gone downtown" is natural and unforced, not the expression of an outsider trying to drop names or coin a phrase that would sound awkward from the lips of a novice (*Hummers*, 77). Joanne Speidel's "rebounding," a compact lyric capturing the precise moment a basketball floats on the rim "until a hand ignites / the spinning ball" and the game "explodes" (*Aethlon* 12.1, 143), does for basketball what Robert Francis's "The Base Stealer" or Robert Wallace's "Double Play" do for baseball. All three poems highlight the energy, balance, and timing involved in their respective moments. All three are essentially genderless.

Though the poems referred to above do not exhibit the four characteristics of women's poetry that Alicia Ostriker identifies, most sports poems by women clearly do. One of these elements, however, the "intimate treatment of the body," requires substantial qualification. Ostriker argues that during the time period she describes, "descriptions of bodily experiences have become the most common sign of female identification in poetry" (118). The key issues she identifies are:

> Looking at and touching oneself, dressing and adorning oneself, menstruation, pregnancy and birth, abortion and rape, the surgeon's knife, the process of aging, the handling of children — because women have traditionally been defined by and confined to the secret gardens of their physical selves, while being forbidden to talk in mixed company about them, they now have much to say [118].

Ostriker's evidence for women's preoccupation with the body is irrefutable, and women's sports poems further solidify the argument. The word *body* itself appears in an incredible number of these works: "the brown arrow of her body" in Patricia Goedicke's "In the Ocean," the "mind returning to the body, the body," in Maxine Silverman's "Hard Hitting Woman: Winning the Serve," "my body / ... moving and beautiful," in Grace Butcher's "Runner Resumes Training After an Injury," "this body / that scythes the water alongside / mine," in Lucia Getsi's "Outswimming," Annette Allen's "Say I consider the mind/body problem," in "A Runner's Quarrel." Individual body parts are also much in evidence, from the joggers' "wounds in knee and back and ankle" in Marge Piercy's "Morning Athletes," to the "swelling of breasts and tingling between thighs" of Nancy Boutilier's "To Throw Like a Boy," and Molly Peacock's assertion in "So When I Swim to Shore" that after swimming she goes home, she lies down, "lips blue, cunt cold, yet / clitoris hard and blue," and she is still alone.[4]

Contemporary women, especially those writing about sport, have been most successful in what Helena Mitchie, in *The Flesh Made Word: Female Figures and Women's Bodies*, labels "re-membering the body," depicting women's bodies as full and complete entities rather than relying on synecdoche to mask reality (97). Unlike the Victorians who depicted women through safe, synecdochal codes—the hair, the wrist, the hand—contemporary women poets in general, and especially those dealing with sport, have striven to depict the whole woman with legs, arms, breasts, bones and stomachs swelled from pregnancy. Paradoxically, the term "re-membering the body" is itself metonymic, describing not the restoration of "members" to a body, but the reconstitution of a unified entity with a personality, a history, and an independent mind.

Although feminist critics disagree on details and emphases, most seek to achieve this wholeness through the rejection of phallocentric attitudes and the received language which has promoted them, the reductive covenants and prescriptions promulgated by the male establishment and stemming ultimately from what Helene Cixous and Madelaine Gagnon refer to as the "self-limiting economy of the male libido" (Jones, 372). In "The Laugh of the Medusa," her writer's manifesto, Cixous argues that women's sexuality, on the other hand, is "cosmic." Its expression, "extraordinarily rich and inventive, in particular as concerns masturbation, is prolonged or accompanied by a production of forms, a veritable aesthetic activity, each stage of rapture inscribing a resonant vision, a composition, something beautiful" (226). Luce Irigaray proclaims that "*Woman has sex organs just about everywhere. She experiences pleasure almost everywhere.... The geography of her pleasure is much more diversified, more multiple in its differences, more complex, more subtle, than is imagined*" (*New French Feminisms*, 103). Trusting these untrammeled impulses promotes the expression of *jouissance*, the pleasure which arises from what Cixous calls "writing the body" (225).

Cixous's injunction that woman must "put herself into the text—as into the world and history—by her own movement" (226) combined with numerous references by Irigaray, Monique Wittig, and others, to "play," "bliss," and "spontaneity," especially in the overall context of "writing the body," would seem to be a compelling prescription for women writing poems about sport. Unfortunately, such does not seem to be the case. While explicit references to the body abound in women's sports poems, and while expressions of *jouissance* can be found, most of these poems are either implicit demands to be taken seriously by the male establishment, direct, logical assaults on that establishment, or relatively straightforward declarations of sisterhood growing out of shared (and only occasionally) agonistic sporting experiences. Individual ecstasy, euphoria, or transcendence are eschewed in favor of insight, understanding, and community. Moreover, though some women seem determined to challenge the stereotypes and limitations historically imposed by men on women's sporting activities, they seem reluctant to question some of the assumptions governing the activities they have chosen deliberately to avoid those limitations. Finally, there is scant evidence to suggest that either the language or technique of these poems is in any way less logical or coherent that that found in the poems of the male establishment.

Generally women's poems directly and deliberately confront the phallocentric control of sport which has either barred them as participants or made the cost of participation so high that the real agon became more social than athletic. The villains in these pieces are the fathers, husbands, coaches, brothers and fans who either deny women access to sport or challenge the identity of those who participate. These poems illustrate Bandy's point that sport cannot be used to affirm a woman's femininity. The phrase "you throw like a girl," for example, appears with slight variation in at least four of the poems I examined and makes explicit the paradoxical role women play in sports.

The operative trope in these poems of protest is restriction, prohibitive rules or boundaries as summed up in Grace Butcher's title, "Girls Didn't Do That," or Judith Wright's observation in "Sports Field" that the children's day is "measured and marked" (*Collected Poems*, 206) by those controlling the events. Often, and most tellingly, restriction takes the form of binding or masking in an effort to disguise a young woman's physical maturation. Linda Mizejewski learned to hold the glove against her chest to "stop / my breasts," and hid her hair beneath her cap to make herself look more like the boy her father longed to play with. Cynthia McDonald's eponymous lady pitcher secures her breasts in netting hidden beneath her uniform when she's on the mound. Off the field, she further denies her gender by not giving in to suitors, afraid that "yielding means / Being filled with milk and put on / the shelf" (*[W]HOLES*, 30). Nancy Boutilier's persona in "To Throw Like a Boy" speaks openly of "unsexing" herself, which was relatively simple in early adolescence, but eventually became impossible when "the swelling of breasts" and other physical manifestations of maturity put her "at war with my body" (*According to Her Contours*, 51). The symbolic maiming described in these poems brings to mind the myth of the Amazons cutting off one breast in order to more effectively pull their bows. The outrage implied in the references is the first step toward the "re-membering" referred to above. The breast in this case is, itself, a metonym, which stands for a woman's identity, not merely a part of the body as a whole.

An interesting variation on the breast-binding motif occurs in a poem entitled "Wings" by Nancy Carter. Inspired by the performances of the women in the 1984 Olympics, Carter's speaker describes her transformation into a winged creature that soars "past pain, past the tired earth." After vicariously participating with the women athletes in the Olympics, the woman in the poem notices the sudden appearance of "buds" on her shoulders. She devises ways of "looking into mirrors" (*Atalanta*, 2) to monitor their growth. She contrives to be last in lines so that no one else will see them, and describes two kinds of pain associated with their growth. First is the physical pain, but along with it, the pain of containing what she knows about herself until the point at which she can no longer be understood as what she was before. She has become someone entirely different.

What is intriguing about this process is that each step of the process parallels a young woman's physical maturation, her fascination with and developing pride in her breasts. In "Wings" the young woman's new appendages are, in fact, symbolic breasts, a doubling of her womanhood, a repudiation of those who would deny her identity, and a reinforcement of her kinship with the women whose athletic achievements have energized her.

In the same manner that Carter's poem repudiates the restrictions and symbolic mastectomies described by so many women, Barbara Crooker in "Starving for the Gold" pursues them to their coldly logical conclusion, the total obliteration of self, literal as well as figurative. In order to conform to expectations, and perhaps win the gold medal, the gymnast in this poem worked to "look like a boy, no breasts / or butt." She steeled herself not to feel pain, then "not to feel / anything at all." Her ideal was "a body light and fluid / as a pink satin ribbon / floating in the wind." Her ultimate desire was to "let go / the bounds of earth" (*In the Late Summer Garden*, 16), a goal which she literally achieved in death. "Starving for the Gold" lacks a clearly identified villain. No parent, coach, or teammate demands that the gymnast create for herself a "body bound as Victorian women in whalebone." Instead, Crooker's gymnast is a perfect example of Foucault's "docile body," a victim of self-surveillance driven by demons she has internalized, what Sandra Bartky terms "technologies of femininity" which control women by generating in them a "pervasive sense of bodily deficiency" ("Foucault," 71). In her resolution not to be a "loser," the gymnast suffers from what Carole Oglesby calls "androgen poisoning," the pervasive influence in sports of males' preoccupation with competition, aggression, and violence (*Sport*, 242).

Telling the truth about anatomy unites women's sports poetry with women's poetry at large. But it is the one attribute among the four Ostriker cites which links the poetry written by women about sport to that which has been written by men. Bodies and body parts are ubiquitous in men's sports poetry, especially that drawn from boxing or football. Lucilius' boxer has given up his physical identity to his sport. He has become unrecognizable to the point that he has lost his inheritance. Ron Smith's noseguard lives amid

> the jumbled debris
> of knees, of bodies writhing
> on the earth, gnawed
> cleats eye-high raking
> on columns of leg, elbows
> in the air like grenades.
> ["Noseguard," 61]

In the stinging shower after the game, "hearts throb all over my flesh" Smith writes. David Hilton's aging basketball player goes up for a jump shot and feels his legs give way when he lands (*Huladance*, 58). Donald

Hall, in "Couplet," writes about Old Timers' Day in Fenway Park, and remarks that on the playing field "we observe the ruin / of even the bravest body..." (*Fathers*, 143).

Men have known since they began writing poems about sport that the body they celebrate will ultimately betray them, and women, who have, according to Ostriker, been "raised up to be narcissists" know they are in "a game every woman ultimately loses" (119). When the game becomes literal, the stakes become even more evident, as when Janice Lynch in "Sixty-Four Caprices for a Long-Distance Swimmer" describes older women nude in the locker room. Many of them exhibit physical disabilities and scars, and in their decrepitude she recognizes how she, too, will grow old. Echoing this theme but adopting a radically different point of view, Carolyn Kremers in "When I Am 98" imagines herself as a nonagenarian recalling the specific details of her daily run in college. At first glance the poem seems, in its specificity and exuberance, to be a naïve celebration of youthful vitality, until the speaker says she wants to remember stretching out "like a corpse" (*A Whole Other Ball Game*, 108) in the weight room, a hint that even as a young woman she recognized that her activities and their accompanying noises were delusional stays against the press of mortality. Even as a young woman Kremers knows that her older self will recall that at the peak of athleticism she was only intoxicated with her youth and its flimsy assurances.

Like Clarissa in Pope's "Rape of the Lock" women are particularly adept at recognizing the folly in others who place too much stock in physical attributes. "Frail beauty must decay," and even the strongest body succumbs to injury, disease and aging. In a finely turned sonnet entitled "Golden Warriors End Year with Big Loss," Marilyn Taylor admonishes a young football player (her son?) that sometime it will occur to him that his body is softening, that his "hamstrung legs" will "race / right past" his "final season" (*Poetry*, July 1995, 222). Her theory seems to be that the boy's immediate loss will somehow be offset by the spectre of inevitable, total defeat.

Not only does the body age, it breaks down, as three poems on running make clear. Two of them actually link aging with injury. Fleda Brown Jackson explains in "A Jogging Injury" that the message of the gods who had interrupted her run at midstride is not necessarily shocking because her injury contributes to a pattern of aches and pains which dog her at this point in her life. Her turned ankle is merely one more reminder of the need for her to revise her youthful dreams which enter her thoughts "like dried flowers / too tender to touch." Her pain is, therefore, a "godsend" (*This Sporting Life*, 98). Nina Nyhart in "The Runner" describes a marathoner about to win a race but he knows that nearing the finish some accident could still interfere, some breakdown of his body occur, so

> that when he tries to lift his sneakered foot
> the heavy jaws will clamp down on his heel.
> [*Poetry*, Jan. 1988, 141]

For this runner, however, the running, the flirtation with injury, is the only thing in his life that allows for the possibility of risk. Paradoxically, the threat of injury energizes the runner's life as a whole, not just the competition. Without the inherent risk competition would serve little purpose.

A more somber treatment of a running injury occurs in Annette Allen's "A Runner's Quarrel," in which the poet rehearses the Cartesian mind/body split and concludes that it is difficult to wax philosophical while she lies on the ground with a fractured collar bone. In a conclusion very similar to but darker than Fleda Jackson's, Allen argues that her injury, though it will heal, has put the mark of death upon her, hanging "like a clump of red berries" (*Southern Poetry Review*, Fall 1993, 60).

Finally, in Diane Wakowski's "Red Runner," the middle-aged speaker encounters a flashy young runner, dressed in red. The situation is rather common in women's sports poems. A speaker recognizes a bond between herself and the athlete, a kinship, sisterhood seen in a glance. But in this instance, the red runner's panache evokes in the older woman a recognition of her fading vitality. At her age, Wakowski argues, even the flamboyant symbol of vitality reminds her "not so much a change, as a proof of / sameness" (*Emerald Ice*, 305). What this "slow mover" identifies as "sameness" is the burden of mortality, which haunts any self-conscious organism, male, female, athlete, poet, or any combination of the roles with gender.

Clearly, insofar as emphasis on the body is concerned, women's sports poems are as fixed on things physical as "mainstream" women's poetry, but they are no more body-centered than men's sport poetry. There is a significant difference in the two approaches when competition enters the picture. As an antidote to "androgen poisoning" women offer poems which celebrate community and sisterhood through sport. The sports they most often choose as subjects— swimming and running dominate — lend themselves to advocacy of these values. Swimming, more often a recreational activity than a sporting contest, provides what Sharon Carson and Brooke Horvath isolate as the key "female" (if not strictly feminist) elements in Maxine Kumin's "Morning Swim":

> a dilution of egotism and absence of competition and violence; and affirmation of joy, health, self, and communion; the portrayal of a positive body image; a freedom from stifling regimens or fears of failure; a peaceful coexistence with and love for the other... ["Women's Sports Poetry," 120]

While none of these pleasures is exclusive to swimming, and there are motifs in many swimming poems— the eroticism associated with sharing a warm pool with another, for example — that Carson and Horvath omit (quite appropriately in this case, since Kumin's swimmer is alone), their list explains the appeal of water. It also illustrates the stark contrast in gender-based attitudes toward sport. One would be hard-pressed to concoct a list less descriptive of "mansport" than this one.

Other swimming poems which illustrate the applicability of Carson's and Horvath's elements include Kumin's "To Swim, To Believe," in which the speaker gives her body to the "king-sized pool of waters," and becomes a "supplicant," a "bride" (*House, Bridge, Fountain, Gate,* 31); Patricia Goedicke's "In the Ocean," in which she, her sister and her mother "swim together as one" (*This Sporting Life,* 22); and the erotically-charged "Competition" by Mariah Burton Nelson. In this last, the speaker asserts, " I like to swim naked, / I like to swim fast," and admits to her companion:

> that I need you
> you can tell by my stroke
> by the way that I breathe

> that I need your stroke
> your breath
> that to be my best I need you
> swimming beside me
> [*Are We Winning Yet?*, npn]

One final example of a swimming poem includes both a rather smug reference to redressing past indignities suffered at the hands of dominant males, and a charitable gesture promoting reconciliation. In "Sixty-four Caprices for a Long-Distance Swimmer: Notes on Swimming 100 Miles," Janice Lynch swims past men to demonstrate her strength — "after years of /'throwing like a girl'" (*Beloit Poetry Journal*, 37, 32). Later, however, she helps a paralyzed man, imagining that some of her strength is transferred to him through the water. Lynch ends her piece with a declaration of unity similar to those referenced above. When she swims she declares herself "pure strength and energy" (32). Even the hint of the competitive edge, the residue of resentment which obtrudes on the swimmer's immersion experience, is ultimately washed away by her absorption in the flow.

Swimming, then, provides the ideal medium through which "positive" values are promoted in sport. And if ecstasy derives from what Ostriker describes as "the dissolving of boundaries between individual selves, and at especially blissful moments, the elimination of distinctions between human and nonhuman existence" ("In Mind," 124), one could argue that *jouissance* could be a part of its appeal, but none of the experiences described in these poems achieves "the stage of rapture inscribing a resonant vision" that Cixous invokes.

Among the running poems, Marge Piercy's "Morning Athletes" provides the best example of community and sisterhood. The "athletes" of the title are two frumpy suburbanites, well into middle age, who meet mornings to jog, in their outfits gleaned from bins at second-hand stores, running side-by-side, in stark contrast to the packs of men in their expensive jogging suits. The two women respect each other, care for each other's art, and enjoy not so much the exercise itself, but the opportunity to be together in a way that encourages them to take in the natural world. They never compete, just "talk and pant, pant and talk / in the morning busy together" (*Circles On the Water*, 254).

IV. Pulling Together

The idea of Stephanie Plotin's "Marathoner," the escape from suffocating, unnatural restrictions to a prelapsarian freedom in nature, recapitulates the liberation from phallocentric, capitalistic shackles advocated by Cixous and her colleagues. But even if one agrees with basketball player Nancy Neremberg that sweating is comparable to orgasm, "like a climax, ... a faucet turning on, a rush" (Nelson, *The Stronger Women Get*, 37), and notes that only when her sweat flows "like sweet water" (*Crossing*, 35) does Plotin's runner "feel real," the poetry does not explode with a sense of *jouissance*. It limps. Grace Butcher's "Runner Resumes Training After an Injury" resonates with a much stronger sense of liberation and rightness with the world. Her runner, flush with the enthusiasm of recovery, and feeling at the exact center of things, has "the grass, the sky, and [her] body / in between, moving and beautiful" (*Before I Go Out on the Road*, 32).

Other expressions of such centeredness and well-being occur in Karen Volkman's "The Pregnant Lady Playing Tennis" and Maxine Silverman's "Hard Hitting Woman: Winning the Serve," both testaments to the competence and power of a woman at the top of her game, and highly competitive, although the former ends with a suggestion that the pregnant woman is at the end of her patience. After playing as if her racquet were a magnet for the ball, she smacks "a crazy slam past the net: past the lines, / past the out zone, past the court's steel network wall" (*Crash's Law*, 61). While these tributes to athletic prowess are successful (perhaps because they have the competitive edge), other blatant declarations of liberation and sisterhood are more polemics than poems. Laurel Starkey's "Women Who Run" and Barbara Lamblin's "First Peace" are good examples. Justice and sincerity notwithstanding, poems which conclude with "These free spirits have found a common foothold / in womankind" ("Women Who Run," *Crossing*, 271) and the summative "feminine power" ("First Peace," *Crossing*, 70) might succeed as manifestos, but not art.

Eminently successful are two poems which at first glance seem to appropriate the competitiveness and aggression common to competitive sport among males. Both Tess Gallagher's "Women's Tug of War at Lough Arrow" and Anita Skeen's "Soccer by Moonlight" describe genuine agonistic struggles with winners and losers. With husbands and children looking on, Gallagher's women pit strength against strength until one side gives in. Skeen's soccer players go at it against the back-drop of the "bloodshot horizon" until one player, her leg "like a hammer swinging" (*More Golden Apples*, 23), slams home the winning goal. Victory seems to be the critical factor in both poems, but Gallagher and Skeen essentially deconstruct their respective contests by making the aftermath gained through vigorous competition more important than the competition itself. Both poems end with the participants embracing. In "Tug of War," one team gives up, letting the rope run slack, free, but immediately they are again taken up in the arms "of those who held them, not until, but so / they gave" (*Amplitude*, 44). Their opposition, the giving of themselves, has led to both teams' giving up in celebration of unity.

Until the last three words of the poem, "Soccer by Moonlight" might very well be about men. Those last words, "the women embrace," reveal that this is indeed a poem about women. The "subversive" message of the poem becomes startlingly clear if one adds only two letters to those words, altering *the* to *their*. The poem would then become a rather conventional, though sweetly lyrical, depiction of men competing with their docile wives on the sideline. Only their women embrace at the end. But Skeen draws in the reader, creates the necessary tension the contest generates, and only after the match is settled reveals that the participants were women. "We can do it, too," the poem implies, but after the grass stains, the bruises and strained knees, we embrace. We don't glare at one another, walk sullenly off the field, or, at best, ritually shake hands.

Both "Women's Tug of War" and "Soccer by Moonlight" represent a challenge to the patriarchal, phallocentric sports world, the transformation of the agon prescribed by Birrell and Theberge. Carson and Horvath further illustrate the way in which women's conceptions of sport differ from men's through the opposition of pairs of poems written by both. Their comparison clearly demonstrates that in the poems they choose women advocate community, freedom, and peaceful coexistence, while the poems by men promote control, restriction and competition. What Carson and Horvath do not point out is that the best sports poems by men balance portraits of repression and macho glory with what Seamus Heaney calls "the redress of poetry," the niggling question that goes against the grain, that, reduced to its simplest form, asks, "What am I doing here?" or, "What is the point of all this?" (*Redress*, 1–16). Examples of this critical edge occur in Gary Gildner's portrait of the sadistic coach Clifford Hill in "First Practice," and in Dave Smith's speaker in "The Roundhouse Voices" who asks his surrogate-father uncle from whom he had learned baseball, "What good did all those hours of practice do?" (*Goshawk, Antelope*, 101). Even macho James Dickey questioned whether Vince Lombardi, the celebrated Green Bay Packers coach, made the men who followed him

> Figments overspecialized, brutal ghosts
> Who could have been real
> Men in a better sense?
> ["For the Death of Lombardi," 117]

Male poets, those who have undergone brutal two-a-days in August, know that football is death-haunted, that boxing is atavistic, that childhood memories of baseball are romanticized, and that the body ultimately betrays us.

Sports poems by women are largely devoid of nostalgia and hagiography. The history simply isn't there yet, and as many "heroes" are disparaged as praised. Mother/daughter, mother/son poems are scarce. And most women, preoccupied with bringing down barriers, flush with their hard-won victories and the freedom they have demanded, have not (with one or two notable exceptions) stopped to question the enterprise itself. Why the long hours of practice to perfect a gymnastic routine, the wear and tear on knees that running exacts, the loyalty to teammates who have nothing in common other than getting together once a week in the summer to play softball?

Brandi Chastain and her teammates, and every woman quoted in this chapter, provide all the evidence necessary to prove that women don't kick, run, throw or write "funny." Their performance on the field or on the page needs no parenthetical qualification or asterisk. The games in both instances are different from men's games, but both can boast of participants who have resisted marginalization, transformed perceptions and expectations, and demanded that they be seen as complete human beings.

V

Small Balls, Microcosmic Courts, and Squared Circles

Poems About Golf, Racquet Sports, and Boxing

For every sport, game, or recreational activity, from tiddly-winks to mumbletypeg to sky-diving, there is a poem. While no "minor" sport has drawn the attention of poets to the degree that baseball, football and basketball have, there is a considerable body of material about some of them, enough to make analysis of poetry about golf, racquet sports (along with handball), and boxing worthwhile. These poems not only define the essence of the sports they depict, the best of them succeed in conveying what Seamus Heaney calls "the pleasure and surprise of poetry, its rightness and thereness" (*Redress*, 192).

Given the wealth of prose dedicated to golf and the accolades it has garnered, it is surprising that relatively few poems deal with it. According to Plimpton's "Small Ball Theory," the quality of literature about a given sport correlates directly with the size of the ball it employs, "the smaller the ball, the more formidable the literature" (13). In addition to the size of its ball, golf, according to Plimpton, has generated a large body of "superb books" owing to the very nature of the game itself. For the golfer, "the bad shot so surely in the future [is] conducive to the state of contained melancholy that so often produces first-rate writing" (13). Golf boasts a pastoral heritage much more genuine and of significantly longer duration than that of baseball. The game's etiquette enforces silence, and creates the potential, at least, for meditation. It's also individualistic, almost to the point of solipsism. But these characteristics have generated only a small corpus of poems. One reason for this neglect is that until recently the game has been, with some notable exceptions, an adult game, not at all productive of the parent/child relationships that pervade so much of baseball poetry. Then there is a taint of elitism articulated so well in Sarah H. Cleghorn's ditty "The Golf Links," in which the children laboring in the mill can look out from their stations at the looms and view the men at play on the links.

An even stronger condemnation appears in John Updike's "Golfers," in which he calls them "one-gloved beasts in cleats" whose wealth has been amassed through the exploitation of the poor. But the sestet in Updike's sonnet turns from sociology to eschatology when his speaker records the exultant golfers' transition from bourbon-breathing athletes to "mere men," shrunken from the shower, their genitals hanging "dead as practice balls." Stripped of the bravado borne of affluence and power, they confront what Ernest Becker terms their creatureliness, the unavoidable fact of their mortality, the horror of "the last hole" (*Collected Poems*, 133).

Updike's point of view in "Golfers" is curious, given his appreciation for golf, particularly its aesthetic appeal. His speaker, apparently an employee of a golf club, hears the group's clattering approach down the stairs leading to the locker room, and expresses dread for the arrogant clients whose presence assures his employment. But the poem illustrates how the same individual who gave us Rabbit Angstrom's perfect golf shot in *Rabbit Run*, one of the quintessential moments in all of sport literature, can be critical of the elitism the game promotes, even though he loves the game itself.

"Golfers" reveals one other persistent theme. Literature about golf is as death-haunted as that about football. Though literature about football focuses on adolescence, the necessary violence of the sport taints it with the smell of death. Golf, on the other hand, has tended to be the sport of old men. Consequently much of its literature chronicles the death of the duffer out for one final attempt to shoot his age. Often, especially in fiction, the death takes on comic overtones. Do the remaining members of the foursome finish out the round after their long-time companion has failed to negotiate the ultimate hazard? Who inherits the regular tee time?

A poem which mixes the suggestion of elitism with the odor of death is William Matthews's "Caddies' Day, the Country Club, a Small Town in Ohio." Noting that he and his fellow caddies had the course to themselves on Mondays, since "even the rich work" then, the speaker admits that the caddies' idea of the rich in the small Ohio town "was Buick dealers we resented / for their unappeasable daughters" (*Foreseeable Futures*, 13). The speaker establishes that elitism in this case is a relative term, but his first direct encounter with death, when Bruce Ransome

> came up
> from the bottom of the pool
> like a negative rising in a tank,
> his body clear, dead, abstract,
> [13]

is unalloyed by geographic location or socio-economic status.

Matthews deftly shifts tenses to allow him to register the young caddy's nausea and bewilderment in the past tense:

> there I was, green as the sick
> and dying elephant in the Babar
> book I thought I had outgrown.
> [14]

He then shifts to the on-going present of memory to depict the stock response the "lucky," who have thus far escaped death, offer up to bolster their own courage. But luck for Matthews seems to involve not ease and freedom, but a bartering of misfortunes:

> Do you want my premature stroke?
> Do I want your retarded child?
> [14]

And the scant consolation the poet tenders involves immersing oneself in the grind of day-to-day work, "one long Monday to the next" (15). Anchoring the work-week to Mondays recalls the title of the poem, the anticipated day off for the caddies, "loopers," for whom work literally meant trudging in circles.

A more personal treatment of the death theme occurs in Cary Waterman's "Last Game," an elegy for a father whose clubs appear at his daughter's door post mortem. The poem, which carries the potential for being terminally maudlin, is rescued by the poet's attention to concrete detail and her reluctance to eulogize. The date of the father's last golf round is stamped on the course ticket attached to the bag. The speaker's son finds in a pocket "the bandaid you kept for blisters," a driving glove, both useless during the last game because "Nothing could protect you then." The poem ends with the grandson examining the sand wedge, a club he has never seen. But instinctively he knows,

> This is the club for difficult places
> for the ball will elude you,
> your strokes slipping down between grains of sand.
> [*When I Looked Back*, 70]

Waterman never abandons the methodical inventory of equipment. She maintains fidelity to the game's essentials while at the same time intimating its applicability to the broader human condition.

Golf has undergone an amazing transformation in the last decade, a democratization leading to the inclusion not only of large elements of the middle class, but of ethnic minorities as well. While the success of the PGA's campaign (carried largely on the back of Tiger Woods) to bring minority children into the game remains to be seen, a quick drive through any suburban/rural area of the country will demonstrate that golf is no longer the exclusive pursuit of doctors, lawyers, and other professionals. Country clubs in many parts of the United States have become truly *country* clubs. And few municipal courses are suffering for want of customers. Despite its elitist traditions, golf, perhaps more than any other sport, lends itself to democratization. The handicap system allows golfers at all skill levels to compete. Moreover, golf is the only sport I know in which a journeyman player can in any given round make a shot that any PGA Tour player would envy.

Dave Smith's "First Tournament Learning Experience" capitalizes upon the way luck sometimes triumphs in this most maddening of games. Following his club pro's instructions, Smith's speaker positions his "feet, hands, cock of chin," in the prescribed manner. He thinks he knows his opponent, but "the little bastard" sticks close for nine holes with "daffy chips, hundred yard irons played / maddening as a boy with his dick up, down, up / down." On a par three the speaker has "almost knocked it in" when his opponent's "scuffed wobbly crier dribbles up," drops in, a "plop audible as halves of breaking wedge whiff / past unyielding oak, and memory's kiss, her handshake" (*Fate's Kite*, 12). The speaker's good round, ruined by his opponent's uncanny shots and the rub of the green, at first seems to merit memory's kiss, but recognizing his penchant for bad luck, the speaker quickly qualifies kiss to mere handshake.

While golf poems, most sports poems for that matter, rely for effect on synecdoche (golf is *like* life), tennis and other racquet sports are played out microcosmically. The game *is* life. In David Allan Evans' "The Zen of Racquetball," for example, the relaxed, focused racquetballer watches the ball "flying back and forth through the white- / walled universe" (*Aethlon* 12.1, 140). More than in any other sports, the "charmed space" in these games controls and dominates play. Whereas in baseball, football, and basketball foul lines or boundaries occasionally determine outcomes, in tennis the line is as much an opponent as the person across the net. In baseball a player can hit foul balls indefinitely and not lose, and baseball's most exciting moments occur when fair balls go beyond the field's boundaries. Offensive players in football can even turn out-of-bounds plays to their advantage, and though basketball is more restricted than baseball or football, its limits are more vertical than horizontal, controlled by gravity more than paint. A basketball game in which the success or failure of each possession was determined by boundary lines would be unthinkable. The spatial restrictions of tennis are even more evident in handball, where the space is smaller, and in racquetball, in which the space is so compressed, so focused, that while play continues neither player nor the ball *can* go beyond the court's confines.

In Maxine Kumin's "Prothalamion" as a husband and wife play tennis each improves the other. The game takes on a life of itself, becomes almost automatic, their universe becoming "contracted to the edge of the dividing line" (*Privilege*, 59). As her husband serves, the wife describes herself positioned "in the square I live in" (*Privilege*, 65). She *lives* inside the confines of the court, locked and connected to her opponent/partner. The game is not a part of her life, from which she can take away memories or lessons for later application. It *is* her life, bounded by lime, which, especially since it is linked through rhyme with *time* in the closing couplet, suggests death and decay, ultimate boundaries.

In "The Pregnant Lady Playing Tennis," to which I referred in the previous chapter, the confines of the game become a metaphor for the limitations imposed by pregnancy, and, by extension, through gender itself. The "lady" is quite skilled, with a "knowledge of speeds and angles / arcs and aims," yet onlookers are torn between anxiety about her safety and annoyance that this distracting exhibition is taking place in their presence. Perhaps sensing their anxiety, the woman, after displaying her mastery, "braces in the pure sensation of her game," and sends a "crazy slam past the net: past the lines, / past the out zone, past the court's steel network wall" (*Crash's Law*, 61). Following the tight control she had exhibited, the deliberate "crazy slam" becomes a personal statement, a protest, against the mandated boundaries of the game, the limited perspectives of the spectators, and most of all, the confines of her own life, the temporal and physical restrictions imposed by pregnancy.

Like golf, racquet sports appeal to the aging athlete. Consequently, many of the poems about them equate performance on the court with performance in life. Some athletes, like Paul Petrie's tennis player in "The Old Pro's Lament," resolve to "play the game purely" (*A Literature of Sports*, 485), as does Evans's racquetballer, in "The Zen of Racquetball," who meditates on the court and thinks of the ball "growing bigger and bigger as it comes / back to me" (*Aethlon* 12.1, 140). Others, such as Galway Kinnell's players in "On the Tennis Court at Night," use tennis as a vehicle to rage against the dying of the light. For Kinnell, the tennis court offers "pure / right angles and unhesitating lines / ...where every man grows old." His players literally confront approaching darkness and a gathering snowstorm. In this impossible scenario they swing where the ball could be, as

> The snow blows down
> and swirls about our legs, darkness flows
> across a disappearing patch of green-painted asphalt
> in the north country, where four men,
> half volleying, poaching, missing, grunting

begging mercy of their bones, hold their ground,
as winter comes on, all the winters to come.
[*Mortal Acts*, 28]

Governed by pure right angles, the boundaries that are for some "the only / lines of justice" they have known, the men struggle not to submit to current conditions. Knowing that the dark, the wind and the snow are precursors of "all the winters to come," they are like Updike's golfers, poised on the brink of that last hole, the unavoidable abyss of death.

In Stephen Dunn's "Day and Night Handball," the conceit which relies on compression reaches its ultimate expression. In Dunn's poem, rather than having the contest's implications slip into the real world, the world is invited onto the court, the game played "day and night," with

shots so fine
and perverse they begin to live

alongside weekends of sex
in your memory.
[*New and Selected Poems 1974–1994*, 44]

The world in this poem is contracted in a way that John Donne would have applauded, so that "all the time / the four walls around you" are "creating the hardship, the infinite variety" (45). Like the racquetball player in "The Zen of Racquetball" and Paul Petrie's "old pro," Dunn's athlete has a sense of himself, "the sense that old men / gone in the knees have," an efficiency born of experience which favors "finesse in place of power" (48). His entire world is bounded by the four walls which force the compression, but at the same time create the infinite variety enjoyed by someone at home with his body and the conditions under which it operates.

One would think that the compactness, the inescapability of the boxing ring would loom as a significant factor in poems about boxing, but it does not. Unlike virtually every other sport analyzed in this study, boxing has provided few participants (Muhammad Ali notwithstanding) who have written poems about their experiences. Poets who have been in the ring at all have fought briefly in their youth, and if they have continued boxing, it has been as a conditioning exercise rather than competition.

There is little sense, then, of compression or entrapment in boxing poems. Lou Lipsitz in "To a Fighter Killed in the Ring" alludes to it by deconstructing the myth that boxing provides an escape from "the brief truth of poverty" (*A Literature of Sports*, 512) that has motivated so many athletes. The brutal truth of Lipsitz's poem is that boxers, whether motivated by a need to better themselves or by internal demons, end up not as role models but as cautionary tales.

Dave Smith, in "Blues for Benny Kid Paret," names the fighter Lipsitz was most likely eulogizing. Although many boxers have died in the ring, Paret was literally beaten to death on national television by Emile Griffith on March 24, 1962. Since that night he has become a symbol of the violence and brutality that is so much a part of boxing and that constitutes a major theme in poems about the sport. In "Blues..." Smith parallels Paret's brutalization with his own suffering resulting from an attack by a swarm of wasps when he was eleven. The stinging left welts and swelling, so that the boy's face looked like a beaten fighter's, but the emotional scars left by the attack were greater than the physical suffering. For years Smith's speaker has looked for signs, "anything for the opening, the rematch I go on dreaming" (*Cumberland Station*, 23). It's not revenge on the wasps he seeks, but some retribution, compensation for the pain he suffered. Driving alone at night, his "load of darkness like the ring no one escapes" (23), he invokes Paret, recalling the radio's voice reporting the fighter was down. And he will not get up, will not offer the speaker the sign he seeks, even a glimmer of hope. Ironically, the speaker, in effect, incorporates Paret's pain into his own burning memory, conflating his own blind careening into a wall, as a result of the wasp attack, with Paret's collapse in the ring. Rather than taking from Paret the sign he seeks, the speaker compounds his own pain by making Paret a participant in his childhood suffering.

Like golf, boxing has inspired a substantial body of prose, both fiction and non-fiction, from Jack London through Joyce Carol Oates. Almost without exception this literature stresses brutality and corruption. Boxing narratives are salted with criminals and gamblers, crooked managers, racist promoters, and crippled fighters, and they provide, in Chris Messenger's words, "the most durable of naturalistic sports stories in our literature" (95–96).

Many poems about boxing, such as the two discussed concerning

Paret, also focus on physical violence and the potential for brutality, but the cumulative effect of the body of poems comes nowhere close to the overwhelming sense of moral and physical decrepitude conveyed by the fiction. Some of the poems, in fact, present boxing in a positive light, focusing on family relationships and boxing's potential for the display of courage and physical beauty.

The potential for violence and brutality is dealt with in "Boxing Towards My Birth" (*Fishing the Backwash*, 70), where Jack Driscoll's speaker recalls his father's gift of a pair of boxing gloves and that first childhood punch in front of a mirror "aimed so willingly at myself." And Charles Ghigna in "A Fighter Learns of Hands" declares that "hands were not made for hitting," but goes on to say that if they must be used "against another" they must be used properly, their final objective "to paint the canvas red" (*Arete* 2.2, 168). Finally, Alan Dugan's portrait of Hurricane Jackson is a direct descendant of Lucilius's lament about the pugilist who has lost his patrimony after a career of being mauled in competition. Jackson suffers from a broken nose, an eye which cannot focus, and he is deaf in one ear. Because he is scarred and disfigured from years of taking punches, he has retreated to the shadowy corners of his mind. The poem ends with a poignant note that someone else, not the adult Jackson, but his "perfect youth ... triumphs forever / to the statistical Sparta of the champs" (*Poems*, 20), small consolation for one whose body is broken, whose career is at an end.

Surprisingly, many boxing poems include strong family elements, especially father/son relationships, not in a participatory sense as in fathers playing catch with their sons, or the Jack Driscoll piece referred to above, but in a spectatorial mode, as vicarious sharers in the fight game's mystique. This familial motif most often manifests itself in nostalgic evocations of "The Friday Night Fights," the title of a poem by Ronald Wallace in which the speaker recreates the weekly ritual during which he lay on the couch while his father cheered Marciano, Liston, or Patterson from his wheelchair. Bitter, even at ten years old, the boy "counted God" among his enemies for what the deity had done to them. Through all the weekly episodes he and the father "never touched." But during the commercials they would join Gillette in the jingle that urged viewers to "Look sharp! Feel sharp! Be sharp!" communing in their "need for blood" in a way that the mother, busy in the kitchen, never understood.

Those Friday nights, Wallace recalls, were as close as he and his father would "ever get / to love — bobbing and weaving, feinting and sparring" (*The Uses*, 23).

Similarly, "A Radio Summer Evening in Nevada" by Michael Huff self-consciously transforms a March Madison Square Garden bout between Ali and Joe Frazier to a summer night, because his memories of his father's being shirtless, the fragrance of honeysuckle, and the chirring of cicadas are so vivid they overcome temporal reality with physical detail. Three times in the piece Huff insists that he heard the fight on a summer evening, that cicadas, crickets and the scent of honeysuckle coalesce to anchor his memory, even after he had seen the film of the fight, "years later," and had even examined the photographs of the evening taken by Frank Sinatra and featured in a spread in *Life*.

The poem's poignancy derives from the speaker's so clearly identifying his father with Ali, the loser by decision in a particularly brutal fifteen-round fight, but a victim, according to Huff, of corrupt judges. Like Ali, his father was bare to the waist. Just as Ali stood up after a knockdown resting his hand on the ropes, so the father was up after hearing the count of four, unconsciously mimicking Ali's posture, his hand on the kitchen counter. Though Huff goes on to cite the *Life* photographs and the fight film, he never again mentions the father directly. But his final evocation of the original setting combines in his memory the sound of the referee's four count (the radio) with the vermilion of Ali's trunks (film and photographs), and the fans' shouting at ringside blending with the fragrance of honeysuckle and the shrill chorus of cicadas outside his window. The insect chorus celebrates Ali's rising above being "betrayed, beaten, giving way to Frazier," to become at the count of four "the issue of life" in his velvet trunks (*Southern Poetry Review*, Summer 1994, 29). The poet's homage to Ali becomes, then, a subtle tribute to his father who mirrored Ali's rising. One assumes that the father, too, overcame adversity, but even if that was not the case, the moment he rose to his feet in support of Ali continues to be a source of "summer" memories for his son.

Two other domestic poems use boxing as their inspiration, David Allan Evans's "Bus Depot Reunion" and Phillip Levine's "The Right Cross." The first describes a young sailor's returning home to be greeted by his grandfather, who doesn't speak, but who demonstrates his affection by sparring with the young man in what is obviously a long-cherished ritual. Neither man lands "a real / punch," but they duck and counter, jab, until they stop at exactly the same moment and "walk away laughing" (*Train Windows*, 17). Levine's poem, a long one, recounts the speaker's quest for the perfect right cross as he works on the "great sullen weight" (*What Work Is*, 68) of the heavy bag hung from the rafters in his garage.

The workout forms the core of Levine's diurnal record which includes his rising with the sun, exercising, writing, and walking after dinner in the garden before retiring. While hitting the bag he reconstructs the coaching his mentor, Nate Coleman, "the gentlest man I ever knew" (68), provided him as a youth. He imagines his sons cheering him on as they observed his circling of the bag, trying once again at sixty to transform Nate's simple instructions into the same perfect execution that Rabbit Angstrom celebrates in his golf game with Reverend Eccles, a kind of magic which focuses even the smallest of the body's molecules for a powerful instant, before returning to an almost automatic defensive posture. The depth of perfection, the totality of involvement Levine describes is as complete and effective as any summarized in these pages. The poet knows his body would recognize the deep but subtle reverberations that would accompany such a punch. But it does not happen.

At this point in the poem Levine expands his scope to explain the dream that motivates men and boys to enter the ring, a dream in which

> the light
> falls evenly as they move without effort
> hour after hour, breathing easily, oiled
> with their own sweat, fighting for nothing
> except the beauty of their own balance
> the precision of each punch.
>
> [70]

It would seem that Levine himself, by implication, would fall among this group of dreamers, but he denies it, saying in no uncertain terms, "I hated to fight." His hatred stemmed from the fact that there always had to be a winner and a loser, "and I / was the loser" (70) he admits.

Now, nearing sixty, he searches for perfect execution, the visceral and aesthetic satisfaction outside competition. Having earned through his workout the small, ritual rewards of the long bath, the shave, the freshly laundered change of clothes, he gives up, for now, comfortable with his limitations, content to walk in the evening among the flowers and listen to the birds call. As evening closes,

> A dove moans,
> another answers from a distant yard as though
> they called each other home, called each of us
> back to our beds for the day's last work.
>
> [71]

Referring to rest as work serves not so much to characterize sleep as labor since it equates the workout in the garage with the restoration sleep promises. The real work is thus diminished through the comparison and folded into the cycle of the whole, the day fulfilled.

"The Right Cross" is in some ways the perfect sports poem. It includes memories of youthful participation, the potential for the beautiful, the revered mentor whose expectations could never be fully met, fathers and sons, winners and losers, and an assessment of a sport's influence on the inner life of a man at peace with himself. Levine's puncher is the opposite number from Updike's Flick Webb or Heyen's Mantle. He never knew the athletic glory they enjoyed, and was, in fact, "crushed in body and spirit" (70) when he entered the ring. He nevertheless internalized those early lessons and experiences, and at sixty resumed the search for perfection, a bonus for someone who, the poem demonstrates, has discovered the beauty of his own balance.

The poems analyzed in this chapter are representative, not only in the sense that they reveal common attitudes and themes found in the individual sports they portray, but also in the sense that they demonstrate that each sport is defined by the poets who choose to write about it. There are fine poems about wrestling, running, track and field, swimming, hockey, and the numerous "extreme sports" enjoyed by young athletes today. A substantial body of hunting and fishing literature also exists. While it would be possible to define each of these sports by the poems written about it, it would also prove tedious. It is sufficient to note that such poetry exists, and that close analysis of poems dedicated to a particular sport would yield themes and attitudes surrounding that sport similar to the themes and attitudes expressed in poems about the representative sports I have chosen for this chapter.

VI

The Fat Man and
Other Spectators
Poems About Fans

Most sports poetry falls into one of four types: the memory poem, often about a childhood or adolescent experience on the court or playing field; the action poem, one which attempts to capture the mood and movement in a game or particular play; the journalistic poem, which records the achievement of an individual or a team as an event; and the celebratory poem, an effort to preserve for posterity the exploits of an heroic player or team. Obviously, these categories are not mutually exclusive. Some poems spill into two or more categories, and some poems resist categorization. Still others fall into a small but significant class, the spectator poem. Many of our most-anthologized sports poems, from Thayer's "Casey at the Bat" to Updike's "Ex-Basketball Player," feature fans and spectators. Some, such as James Wright's "Autumn Begins in Martin's Ferry, Ohio," forge a direct, causal connection between sport and the emotional health of the community. The sons of steel workers and night watchmen "grow suicidally beautiful" (*Collected Poems*, 113) each football season in what appears to be a vain effort to bolster the town's vitality.

While Wright's speaker "in the Shreve High football stadium" generalizes about sport and life, his musings effectively distance him from the physical locus of the poem. The poem might just as well begin at the poet's desk as he is thinking about the stadium since the action it presents is cyclical and intellectualized. The poems dealt with in this chapter, on the other hand, capitalize upon the immediacy the sporting contest provides and the interaction of the speaker or central figure with other spectators. Consequently, sport provides the pretext for rich and varied analyses of watching.

Unlike most poems examined in this inquiry, the products of poets fifty or younger, the standard for "crowd" poems was set by an older generation of writers, William Carlos Williams, John Updike, and Rolfe Humphries. Their respective poems, "At the Ballgame," "Tao in the Yankee Stadium Bleachers," and "Night Game," anticipate the analyses of spectatorship social scientists have offered as recently as 2001 with the publication of *Sports Fans: The Psychology and Social Impact of Spectators* by Dale G. Pease, Merrill J. Melnick, Gordon W. Russell, and Daniel L. Wann.

"At the Ballgame," in which the crowd is "in detail... / ...beautiful" (*Selected Poems*, 31), also warns that that discrete beauty has the potential for coalescing into a vicious and uniform ugliness, a powerful, many-headed beast of Shakespearean proportions historically responsible for racism, sexism and revolution. Williams celebrates the crowd's idle pleasure, but simultaneously cautions that its thoughtless uniformity could generate hatred and violence, what has come to be euphemistically called "hooliganism." In his "Polo Grounds" Rolfe Humphries makes the same distinction between the crowd as one, which never ages, and the individual in the crowd who "gets older every season" (*Collected Poems*, 84). But his poem focuses on the energy and split-second timing of the players contrasted with the timelessness of the game. "Night Game," on the other hand, explores the effects of the total experience on the mind of the speaker who has brought with him "a pest who insisted on going with me," his own foul mood which dogs him throughout much of the game until it is finally banished and the speaker is allowed to focus on what proves to be a relatively unmemorable game. But the communal experience of the game is cleansing. Walking out onto the field afterward, the speaker, along with other spectators, vicariously becomes "a player," toeing the infield dirt, feeling the outfield grass. His irritability evaporates as he shares the camaraderie of men his age, young servicemen with their dates, "the running kids, and the plodding old men" (103). While Williams suspects the communal spirit, Humphries's speaker celebrates his immersion in the spirit of the community, "this movement" and its attendant music.

In "Tao" Updike's speaker is not so much absorbed into a communal spirit as insulated by the protective envelope the game provides. Players, spectators, the field, are all components of the spectacle enhancing the speaker's isolation from the real world. In the bleachers he can imaginatively fuse the disparate elements of the scene into an imaginative whole, a "stage beast, three folds of Dante's rose, / or a Chinese military hat" (*Collected Poems*, 10).

His musings include one Taoist proverb per stanza, each of which reinforces the speaker's sense of a kind of Keatsian drowsy numbness arising from his experience. The final proverb, which begins the last stanza, asserts that "No king on his throne has the joy of the dead" (10), implying that true freedom derives only from obliteration. Again like Keats, however, who realizes as he toys with the idea of death in order to prolong his vision, that death would obliterate the senses which inspired it in the first place, Updike's speaker rejects the "joy of the dead." "The thought of death is peppermint to you," he says,

> when games begin with patriotic song
> and a democratic sun beats broadly down.
> The inner journey seems unjudgeably long
> when small boys purchase cups of ice
> and, distant as a paradise, experts, passionate and deft,
> wait while Berra flies to left.
>
> [11]

His earlier, intellectualized version of the game gives way to the concrete detail. Proverbs, the deliberate pursuit of enlightenment, and even the statistical obsessions of the "experts" fail in the face of a reality that, ironically, absorbs the speaker in a true experience of the Tao.

Three other poems which make a point of renouncing statistics and history in favor of the total experience of the contest are Danny Sklar's "Red Sox: 12 June, 1988," Tom Clark's "September in the Bleachers," and Kim Addonizio's "Event." Sklar's speaker and his son Max took in all the action at Fenway, the hits, runs, etc., but Max also "loved the crowd," as well as the "rooting, cheering, the lights." Even the ballpark delighted him, its "green steel beams... / the red and blue and green lights on the score / board, the big wave that went around the stadium." In the end, the hits and runs are momentary delights. The speaker admits

"We don't know the statistics or standings." What lasts of the experience is that he and Max know "it is he and I in the crowd, part of something." Similarly, Tom Clark, in "September in the Bleachers," records the immediacy of his experience of a Vida Blue shutout. It is critical to note that his *seeing* the game is what matters, since the poem begins with the speaker in a stadium men's room overhearing groups of men betting on a fight between Ken Norton and Muhammad Ali as they listen to the blow-by-blow on their "tiny radios." Heading back up into the stands, following a detour through the hot dog line, the speaker feels in his heart that Blue will pitch a shutout. Clark's last line contrasts markedly with the mediated experience of the fight fans in the men's room and registers the speaker's absolute delight in the fact that Vida "goes ahead and does it, right before my eyes" (*Blue*, 61).

Addonizio's poem lacks the wonder and unalloyed pleasure of the two baseball pieces, but it does fully render the immediacy of the boxing arena, and it suggests an almost obsessive drive on the part of the fight fan to be a part of the action. Like Sklar, Addonizio ignores what would interest the sportswriter, the fighters' weight division, the weight itself, the winner, even the names of the men in the ring. Instead, she paints the entire scene with a series of deft brushstrokes, like a Leroy Nieman painting. She includes vendors, judges and sportswriters, a photographer, sound pick-ups for satellite television, a minor altercation in the twelfth row, cold water poured down trunks of one of the fighters, the chilled spoon a trainer uses to suppress a mouse, packing all seventeen of her three-line stanzas with visual, auditory and tactile detail. At the end of the twelfth stanza, after the scene has been thoroughly rendered, the poem takes a turn. If you're looking for more than what she's given you so far, the poet says, if you crave record book statistics or need the ring girl to haunt your fantasies, "then you know why you're here" (*Philosopher's Club*, 21). In other words, if you've taken in the spectacle she has presented and want more, if you've vicariously entered the ring with the fighters, then you're hooked, drawn in, "you recognize the roaring in your ears" (21). The sharp details pull the reader in to the point at which Addonizio can recognize him as a kindred spirit. She knows he wants more because she has already demonstrated her own obsessive desire to record the full scene. She hears the ringing in her own ears.

The poet's enthusiasm as spectator and the kinship she implies with other fans, her readers included, supports the argument advanced by the authors of *Sports Fans: The Psychology and Social Impact of Spectators* that sports fandom "satisfies an important social imperative in post-modern society by serving as a unique urban structure whereby strangers assemble not only to be entertained, but to 'engage the other' in meaningful dialogue" (188). Readers of Frederick Exley's *A Fan's Notes* would understand that the term "meaningful dialogue" needs to be taken with a grain of salt. Exley joins a "conclave" of working-class men from Brooklyn in the bleachers at the Giants games. "We were Wops and Polacks and Irishmen out of Flatbush," he writes, "and one mad dreamer out of the cold, cow country up yonder" (133). And they do share a communal vision that in the Giants' performance they were "witnessing something truly fine, ... something truly like art" (133). But, while the group represents a community of sorts, the "meaningful dialogue" is limited to "Take the fucking bum outa deah," and the highest accolade the group could bestow on a player is "Dat guy is a *pro*" (132). Ironically, when Exley ends up sharing seats with the genteel all-American family who refer to the players as "Mr. Gifford" and "Mr. Layne," the result is an anti-community of sorts, one more example of Exley's frustration with the American dream.

More often than not, when poets describe spectatorial communities their involvement is with a single individual who becomes an alter ego, a Doppelgänger who represents a degree of dedication to the game the speaker can only aspire to, or who offers admission to a community much like that of Exley and his Flatbush friends which the poet/speaker cannot embrace. Jim Daniels's focal character in "The Fat Man at the Ball Game" is a true aficionado. He eschews the trappings of fandom, the tee shirts and beer mugs, to concentrate instead on keeping accurate statistics. The poem develops around the speaker's growing fascination and ultimate identification with the fan with "the sweet buffalo face." It is noteworthy, for example, that he records the fat man's absence at one game. By the poem's fourth stanza, the man is "my pal," even though the speaker has never spoken to him, and in one attempt to make conversation, the speaker loses his nerve and heads "for the hot dog stand." Even the speaker's wife notes his near-obsession with the other man, asking, "What is it with you and that fat guy?" and by the penultimate stanza he's saying "Sometimes I feel bloated with everything," and "we've all got / a little weight to lose," thus moving even closer to complete identification. They're both "fans of the game," but the fat man and his pure approach to the game achieve such significance that by the end of the poem the speaker seems more interested in him than the game itself, noting that "Last week I saw him clear his throat / and spit a big hawker" (*Aethlon*, 14.1 [Fall 1996], 70). Like a truly obsessed fan, Daniels's speaker records even the most disgusting physical details in the ordinary life of this inflated "other."

"The Fat Man at the Ball Game" is an unalloyed spectator poem. Though one might infer that it takes place in the old Briggs Stadium, given Daniels's well-documented loyalty to the Tigers, the poem contains no reference to the stadium, the play on the field, or any scores. Similarly, David Allan Evans's "Will You Sign My Brand-New Baseball, Louie," provides no play-by-play description and no score, though it does establish that the game takes place between Kansas City and Boston, and Louie Aparicio is the BoSox shortstop. But "the best thing in my head" about the game for the poet is the drunk in the stands who methodically troops down from the grandstand into the box seats "with amazing / timing" every half inning in order to urge Aparicio to sign his new ball. Aparicio, of course, deftly manages to drop his gaze as he enters the dugout, so the fan is ignored. As the game goes on, the crowd, which includes the speaker, begins to anticipate the drunk's appearance, to identify with him and encourage his efforts, making him a momentary hero, like Aparicio, that they "cheer and cheer and / cheer" (*Train Windows*, 29). Whereas Daniels creates an individual, somewhat spiritual affinity with his Doppelgänger, the crowd in Evans's poem pulls itself together around an amusing fan onto whom they can project their own fantasies of audacious behavior.

"In the Red Seats" by Andrew Hudgins also deals with a drunken spectator, and it has much in common with both Evans's and Daniels's poems. The stadium and the teams involved are unnamed. The only score revealed is 0–0 in the first inning, and the speaker leaves in the fifth inning, so no winner is announced. But Hudgins's speaker rejects the offer of community tendered by one particular fan in the red seats. He is already seated high up in the stadium when "four drunks edge by," requiring him to stand to ease their passage. One of them, his back to the field, mutters, "Great game," as he shuffles by, though the game is barely underway. As their eyes meet, the drunken man begins to fall backward until the speaker reaches out and pulls him upright and their foreheads touch. The drunk's eyes flood with love, and he sobs, "You saved my life, man. / I swear I'll never forget you." The speaker shakes off the gesture of affection. Another man in the group going by raises an eyebrow and shrugs, as if to say, "What are you going to do?" and they all sit down five seats over. But the drunk doesn't forget. As he sits a short distance away, love shimmers and radiates from his face

> like equatorial sunshine,
> the way a lover's face
> illuminates the lover,
> the loved, and the dark world
> in one strange, lucent moment:
> satisfied and thrilled, intense
> and effortless—as God
> regards us every moment.
>   [*Babylon*, 10]

Unable to endure the aftermath of what was an automatic gesture on his part, the speaker gets up and walks out in the fifth inning, reversing the path of his new-found friend, "easing past strangers, / excusing myself" (10). His polite departure contrasts radically with the drunk's entrance, and his reference to fellow spectators as "strangers" even after five innings together in the red seats is tantamount to a rejection of what might be called fanship, which suggests more of a human failing on his part than a serious criticism of easy intimacy fueled by alcohol. The drunk quite obviously will not be his friend for life, but the speaker is incapable of basking in the radiated love even for a few innings.

Sharon Bryan's "Cheap Seats in the Kingdome" also focuses the attention of the speaker on another fan, this one, like the fat man, the object of the speaker's attention. Like the baseball fan in "Red Seats," the speaker here is up so high up "there should be switchbacks" to the climb, and the players on the court below "look like tiddlywinks." The object of the speaker's attention is an angelic young woman who takes a seat with her "cherubic, straight-haired son" (*Objects of Affection*, 3) four rows below. The two bask in the heavenly aura the speaker surrounds them with until they are joined by a "rat-faced man" sloshing beer over his shoes. From that point on the young woman virtually ignores the boy, and the speaker, crestfallen that her illusion is shattered, is left trying to explain the relationship between the seemingly incompatible rat-faced man and the angelic woman. She determines that "what they saw in each other" were "endless days of saving and being saved, / their thin bones crackling like cellophane" (4), a decidedly unsaintly co-dependence. The rarified air of the cheap seats is further contaminated by the appearance of an old, uniformed usher, who makes his way haltingly up the steep stairs monitoring the crowd's behavior. But "no one looks guilty," Bryan writes, so he tries to act as if he wheezed his way to the cheap seats only because he wanted to take a walk, wondering as he crosses to an empty row, what it would be like to dive all the way to the arena's floor. The usher's suicidal thoughts are not really his own, but those the speaker projects, a byproduct of her recent disillusionment.

Things turn around, however, when, breaking with a pattern seen in the poems examined above, the speaker turns her attention to the action on the floor. The Sonics, who were a point behind in the last two seconds, win on a three-point shot from David Thompson. Buoyed by victory, "our spirits / rise to the roof" (4) along with the speaker's rationalization that "Maybe the boy's her / brother," and the cautious observation that "Maybe there's still hope" (4). But the double "maybe[s]" make for a resolution so tentative that even the Sonics' victory can't tip the balance, and the fact that the speaker cannot abandon the woman and the boy, even in the flush of victory, indicates the degree to which their elevation to celestial stature represents an almost desperate search for purity and goodness.

A remarkably similar treatment of spectatorial community, or lack of it, occurs in William Matthews's "Cheap Seats, the Cincinnati Gardens, Professional Basketball, 1959." Like Hudgins and Bryan (with whom he shares his title), Matthews makes a point of his distance from the action, opening with, "The less we paid, the more we climbed" (*Time and Money*, 35). Matthews identifies immediately with a community of sorts, "numerous boys in molt," who share a hormonal drive that sends them in search of companionship, but little else. There is no "we," since the speaker knows "none [of them] by name." He briefly entertains a comparison with the home team, since the Royals, like the young men near the rafters, lost "two nights out of three." He then abandons this tentative comparison, noting that, unlike the players, who at least enjoyed closure, Matthews and his fellow hopefuls "had no result / three nights out of three" (35). Thus the need for heroes. Nights at the arena offered "loneliness / with noise," a condition which momentarily seems to contrast markedly with the loneliness he endures at home "with no clock running down, and mirrors" (35). But this distinction, like his tentative identification with the other young men which he tenders and then rejects, since he knows none of them by name, breaks down. Ironically, as it disintegrates, it confirms the bond among the "boys in molt" that Matthews earlier denied. There is no game clock at home, ticking off the seconds in a finite contest, but Matthews's implicit sense of urgency posits at least an awareness of time passing ("three nights out of three..."), and while the cheap seats at the Cincinnati Gardens lack the mirrors he would confront at home, the "other boys" reflect his image, even though he knows none of their names. What they have in common, however, is loneliness.

Loneliness also dominates Richard Hugo's "Missoula Softball Tournament" in which the poet has returned "to the old ways of defeat" (*Making Certain*, 210), the community softball field where local men, cheered on by their wives, relieve the tensions of the work week through league games. Hugo pays close attention to the game, trying to steal signs, evaluating play and attempting to determine the umpire's tendencies. But while he is obviously interested in the game, most of the poem's emphasis is on the spectators, especially, "the wives, / the beautiful wives," a phrase he repeats with some variation three times in the poem's 34 lines. The "poem goes out to them," in fact. Hugo sees in them a realistic potential for renewed vitality that James Wright's speaker in "Autumn Begins..." can only wish for. Writing about the poem in an essay entitled "The Anxious Fields of Play," Hugo says,

> I sat up in the stands and took note of the spectators as well as the game, of the players' wives and children, of the players from teams not on the field. One night I watched a player's wife with a small child. It was beautiful. *She* was beautiful, a full, warm woman who radiated affection. I imagined myself coming home to her from work tired and putting my head in her lap [*Real West*, 47].

Another wife, who keeps score "with intense dedication," is described as "in her thirties and the mother of three children." Even so, to Hugo, "her flesh looked soft and virginal, like that of a high school girl" (47). The commentary only reinforces what the poem makes clear from the beginning, that the poet, with most of his friends "out of town" and little else to occupy him, intensifies his own loneliness through contrasting it with what he envisions as the fulfilled lives of those around him in the stands.

An altogether different kind of spectator response is made possible through radio and television. This mediated spectatorship was discussed with reference to Ronald Wallace's "The Friday Night Fights" and Michael Huff's "A Radio Summer Evening in Nevada" in the previous chapter. Not surprisingly, the mediated spectator's experience differs from that of the "live" spectator mostly in the degree to which elements of the game being watched or listened to become integrated into the day-to-day lives of the viewers or listeners. Most radio poems feature nostalgia of one form or another. Baron Wormser's "Listening to a Baseball Game," for example, looks back at a boy lying on a bed, reading *Life*, listening to a game from Kansas City. Wormser emphasizes the boy's ability to "see" the game as it's being delivered through the announcer's play-by-play. As the night sounds accumulate around him, the boy quits reading and "lets his feelings glide / With each intent description" (*When*, 5). The boy is mature enough to realize that "comfort is rarely pure," an observation that suggests that if the young man is not experiencing pure comfort at the moment he is not far from it. Robert Gibb's "Listening to the Ballgame" is not so much nostalgic as celebratory. His speaker lies on the couch and listens to the game while his wife "Sings in the kitchen, slicing / Red berries into a bowl." He enjoys a period of "splendid ease," recognizing that even though "So much of what we love takes / Place beyond us" (*Momentary Days*, 16–17), this is one instance in which the beyond is brought near through the magic of radio.

But not all mediated spectator poems are positive, although the game being listened to in Alison Stone's "Nobody Left On" provides such pleasure to the man listening that the poem's speaker, his neighbor, envies his "good sex" until she realizes he is reacting to the play-by-play of a Mets/Dodgers game. Like Gibb's speaker, the man is able to "squeeze such ecstasy / From a scene beyond himself" (*Buffalo Spree*, Summer 1989, 127) and his joy provides one more irritation for the woman suffering through memories of catching grass lice on her honeymoon in Jamaica. Thoughts of her (ex-?) husband still make her skin crawl. Her dog doesn't pay attention to her. Her self-help books are used only to prop up other books on her shelf, and even the fuzz on her blanket "tickles / like the feet of bugs" (107). She concludes that since in baseball "errors are just part of the game," and that "no score is too low to be a victory / If the other team does worse," then "Happiness is relative" (107). Hoping, therefore, to gain some measure of happiness at the expense of her Mets fan neighbor, she screams out, "'Go Dodgers.'"

"Nobody Left On" makes light of its speaker's plight, but, like so much humor, it underscores the seriousness of her desperation. Like most other spectators depicted in these poems, the woman listening through the wall is lonely. In *Soccer Madness*, Janet Lever asserts that "sport promotes communication; it involves people jointly; it provides them with common symbols, a collective identity, and a reason for solidarity" (14). In prose fiction, in television coverage of sports events showing costumed fans who dance and participate in the wave, and even in post-game conversations at offices and cookouts, such communication does take place. But not in the poet's sportsworld. The poet might feel a vague identification with an abstract crowd. He or she might even report a feeling of heightened intimacy enjoyed in sharing a sporting event with a close friend or family member, but for the most part poets are spectators of spectators, themselves detached, analytical, longing, and lonely.

Wrap-Up

My most serious misgiving about offering this volume as a comprehensive treatment of contemporary American sports poetry is that I have not been able to keep up with the volume of poetry published about sport. Even trying to take into account "legitimate" poetry which has been around for a decade or more has proved difficult at times. Significant poetry has been left out, but not ignored. Lawrence Ferlinghetti's "Baseball Canto," for example, might have fit into my final chapter on spectators, but it would have opened up a new theme of broadly political sports poetry which I determined not to treat. More significant are the recently-published anthologies best represented by Horvath's and Wile's *Line Drives* and Noah Blaustein's *motion*, which appeared late in my study's development. I have referenced many of the poems featured in these collections and explicated several which were central to specific arguments, but I lacked the time to analyze either anthology with the thoroughness it deserved.

Similarly, I feel there is much work to be done on single volumes or collections devoted to sport or focused exclusively on one sport by individual authors. Kenneth Koch's *Ko, or a Season on Earth* is a prime example, and three volumes published by McFarland, Tim Peeler's *Touching All the Bases* (2000) and *Waiting for Godot's First Pitch* (2000), and Joseph Stanton's loving tribute to the St. Louis Cardinals, *Cardinal Points*, deserve close attention.

Those gaps in my study notwithstanding, the preceding pages demonstrate beyond doubt that a considerable body of sports poetry exists in our culture, and that that poetry is worthy of serious analysis. What Felix Stefanile has said in a review of *Hummers, Knucklers and Slow Curves*, that the baseball poetry it contains creates "a "high-quality, composite of American culture — the money, grit, glamor, and dross — ... real truths" ("Poetry That Reaches Out," 14), applies equally well to serious poems about football, basketball, or golf.

A. E. Housman, the author of "To an Athlete Dying Young" (probably the most famous sports poem in English literature), asserted that "poetry indeed seems to me more physical than intellectual" (Weinstein, 9), a comment remarkably consistent with Dave Smith's remark in his interview in "Heroes of the Spirit" (*Graham House Review*) that poets "recognize and delight in the grace of the body," and his paraphrase of John Crowe Ransom's statement that a poet must have in the right order "...the head, the heart, and the foot." Add to this the comment by Charles Woodard that "poetry is graceful and rhythmic like athletics ... and it can be muscular and energetic, like athletics (*The Sport of Poetry...*, npn), and all that remains to be considered to solidify the alliance of poetry and sport, are the poems themselves. Dave Smith's own poems treat sporting subjects ranging from baseball to golf with the craft and intensity he brings to any subject. The work of William Matthews, whom no one could label as a "jock poet," provides ample evidence that serious poems can be written about baseball, basketball, golf, and the sports spectator. And the poems of James Wright, Maxine Kumin, and John Updike rival those of Matthews and Smith in variety and intensity.

Still poems about sport lack the attention and appreciation they should be receiving from educated readers, as a recent article in *Golf Magazine* makes abundantly clear. In a regular column, "The Golf Life," entitled in this issue "Poetry in Motion," James Dodson features an interview with our recent poet laureate, Billy Collins, which takes place as the pair are making their way around a golf course. A devotee of the game, Collins tells Dodson, "As far as I know, there's never been a good poem about golf. Or for that matter, any poem about golf that I can recall" (February 2003, 34). There is no reason Collins should be aware of the significant number of good golf poems, but he should at least know the much-anthologized indictment of the leisure class by Sarah Cleghorn, "The Golf Links," and anyone who loves the game should have read Updike's "The Golfers." There is even a poem called "Seaside Golf" by John Betjeman, the poet laureate of England from 1972–1984.

Collins's lack of awareness where golf poetry is concerned is symptomatic of a situation in which sympathetic, eager readers of poetry continue to be kept in the dark about the poetry of sport. It also provides more than ample justification for this study. Careful readers of the poems referenced in these pages will not only be exposed to a rich vein of wonderful poetry, they can also learn a great deal about the sports those poems portray, about the culture in which those sports are played, and, indeed, about poetry itself.

Chapter Notes

Introduction

1. Messenger's Chapter 8 is entitled "Anti-Heroism: The Witness at the Center."

2. See "Bibliography of Primary Works—Anthologies" for a list of anthologies published since 1977.

3. The source for Matthews's assertion is "Dull Subjects," *New England/Bread Loaf Quarterly* 8 (1985), 142–152.

4. For further elaboration of this argument, see my article "Heaney at Play," *Southern Review* 38.2 (Spring 2002), 358–371.

Chapter I

1. Parts of this chapter have appeared in *The Achievement of American Sport Literature: A Critical Appraisal*, ed. W. Lee Umphlett (Teaneck, NJ: Fairleigh Dickinson University Press, 1991) as "'Who the Hell Are You, Kid?': The New Baseball Poem as a Vehicle for Identity," 107–115; and in the introduction to *Hummers, Knucklers, and Slow Curves: Contemporary Baseball Poems*, ed. Don Johnson (Urbana: University of Illinois Press, 1991), xix–xxvii.

2. All three of Francis's poems appear in *The Orb Weaver* (Middletown, CT: Wesleyan University Press, 1948); Welch's "High Jumper" appeared in *Arete* 2.2 (Spring 1985); Kent Cartwright's "Scoring" appeared in *Arete* 1.2 (Spring 1984).

3. See Giamatti, *Take Time for Paradise....* (New York: Summit Books, 1989), Chapter 3, and Messenger (*Sport ... in Contemporary American Fiction*) (New York: Columbia University Pres, 1990), 316–317.

Chapter II

1. This chapter first appeared, in a slightly different version, as "End-Zones Scored with Darkness: The Contemporary American Football Poem" in *Aethlon* 9.2 (1992): 73–90.

2. See Kevin Kerrane, "Reality 35, Illusion 3: Notes on the Football Imagination in Contemporary Fiction," *Journal of Popular Culture* 8.2 (1974): 438–52.

Chapter III

1. Both Harper's and Komunyakaa's poems are collected in *motion,*

ed. Noah Blaustein (Iowa City: University of Iowa Press, 2001).

Chapter IV

1. For a comprehensive application of Birrell's and Theberge's approach to a single piece of literature, see Pirkko Markula, "'I Gotta Do the Marathon': Women's Running as a Truth Game," *Aethlon* 18.1 (Fall 2000): 89–106.

2. Susan Bandy in "The Female Athlete as Protagonist: From Cynisca to Butcher," *Aethlon* 15.1 (Fall 1997): 83–97, also relies heavily on Ostriker's analysis of women poets. Bandy and Anne Darden also integrate Ostriker's observations about women's poetry into the critical apparatus of *Crossing*

Boundaries: An International Anthology of Women's Experiences in Sport (Champaign, IL: Human Kinetics, 1999).

3. Ackerman's poem is collected in *Slam Dunk*, ed. Lillian Morrison (New York: Hyperion Books, 1995); Clifton's poem is collected in *At the Crack of the Bat*, ed. Lillian Morrison (New York: Hyperion Books, 1992); Herport's poem appears in *Aethlon* 4.2 (Spring 1987).

4. Goedicke's, Getsi's and Silverman's poems are collected in *Crossing Boundaries*. Peacock's poem is collected in *The Morrow Anthology of Younger American Poets*, Smith and Bottoms, eds. (New York: Morrow, 1985); for complete references to the poems of Allen, Boutilier, Butcher and Piercy see "Bibliography of Primary Works."

Bibliography of Primary Works

Anthologies

Atalanta: An Anthology of Creative Work Celebrating Women's Athletic Achievement. Sandra Martz, ed. Watsonville, CA: Papier Mache Press, 1994.

Baseball, I Gave You All the Best Years of My Life. Richard Grossinger and Kevin Kerrane, eds. Oakland, CA: North Atlantic, 1977.

The Crack of the Bat. Lillian Morrison, ed. Buena Vista, Burbank, CA: W. D. Publishing, 1992.

Crossing Boundaries: An International Anthology of Women's Experiences in Sport. Susan Bandy and Anne Darden, eds. Champaign, IL: Human Kinetics, 1999.

Full Court: Stories and Poems for Hoop Fans. Dennis Trudell, ed. Halcottsville, NY: Breakaway Press, 1999.

Hummers, Knucklers and Slow Curves: Contemporary Baseball Poems. Don Johnson, ed. Urbana: University of Illinois Press, 1990.

Line Drives: 100 Contemporary Baseball Poems. Brooke Horvath and Tim Wiles, eds. Carbondale: Southern Illinois University Press, 2002.

A Literature of Sports. Tom Dodge, ed. Lexington, MA: D. C. Heath, 1980.

More Golden Apples: A Further Celebration of Women and Sport. Sandra Martz, ed. Watsonville, CA: Papier Mache Press, 1986.

The Morrow Anthology of Younger American Poets. David Bottoms and Dave Smith, eds. New York: Morrow, 1984.

motion: American Sports Poems. Noah Blaustein, ed. Iowa City: University of Iowa Press, 2001.

The Sporting Spirit: Athletes in Literature and Life. Robert J. Higgs and Neil Isaacs, eds. New York: Harcourt, Brace, 1977.

Sports in Literature. Bruce Emra, ed. Chicago: NTC, 1991.

Sports Poems. P. R. Knudson and P. K. Ebert, eds. New York: Dell, 1976.

This Sporting Life: Contemporary American Poems About Sports and Games. Emile Buchwald and Ruth Roston, eds. Minneapolis: Milkweed Editions, 1987.

A Whole Other Ballgame: Women's Literature on Women's Sport. Jolie Sandoz, ed. New York: The Noonday Press, 1997.

Individual Works

Ackerman, Diane. *Lady Faustus.* New York: Morrow, 1983.

Addonizio, Kim. *The Philosopher's Club.* Rochester, NY: BOA Editions, 1994.

Alexie, Sherman. "Native Hero." *Aethlon* 6.2 (Spring 1989).

_____. "Sudden Death." *Aethlon* 6.1 (Fall 1988), 147.

Allen, Annette. *Southern Poetry Review* (Fall 1993), 60.

Behm, Richard. "The Origin and Purpose of Baseball." *Quarterly West* (Spring-Summer 1984), 98–99.

Bettencourt, Michael. "The Freshman Football Game." *Arete* 4.2 (Spring 1987), 97–98.

Bottoms, David. *Armored Hearts.* Port Townsend, WA: Copper Canyon Press, 1995.

Boutilier, Nancy. *According to Her Contours.* Santa Rosa, CA: Black Sparrow Press, 1992.

Bowers, Neal. "Late Innings." *Helicon Nine* 19 (1988), 45.

_____. "Losing Season." *Arete* 3.2 (Spring 1986), 141.

Bryan, Sharon. *Objects of Affection.* Middletown, CT: Wesleyan University Press, 1987.

Butcher, Grace. *Before I Go Out on the Road.* Cleveland: Cleveland State University Poetry Center, 1979.

_____. "Girls Didn't Do That." *Aethlon* 7.2 (Spring 1995), 144–145.

Byrd, Bobby. "One of the Meanings of the 1987 NBA Championship Series." *Aethlon* 5.2 (Spring 1988).

Carlson, Doug. "Russ Joy Little League." *I Hate Long Goodbyes.* Jamestown, NY: JCC Press, 1983.

Cartwright, Kent. "Scoring." *Arete* 1.2 (Spring 1984), 41.

Chappell, Fred. *The World Between the Eyes.* Baton Rouge: Louisiana State University Press, 1971.

Clark, Tom. *Blue.* Los Angeles: Black Sparrow Press, 1974.

Connolly, Jim. "Home Movies." *Arete* 1.2 (Fall 1984), 122.

Corso, Gregory. *Happy Birthday of Death.* New York: New Directions, 1960.

Couto, Nancy Viera. *The Face in the Water.* Pittsburgh: University of Pittsburgh Press, 1990.

Crooker, Barbara. *In the Late Summer Garden.* Middlebury Center, PA: H & H Press, 1998.

Dacey, Philip. *The Boy Under the Bed.* Baltimore: Johns Hopkins University Press, 1981.

Daniels, Jim. "The Fat Man at the Ball Game." *Aethlon* 14.1 (Fall 1996), 70.

DeFoe, Mark. "Hoop League." *Arete* 3.2 (Spring 1986), 91.

Dickey, James. *The Central Motion: Poems, 1968–1979.* Middletown, CT: Wesleyan University Press, 1983.

_____. *The Eyebeaters, Blood, Victory, Madness, Buckhead and Mercy*. New York: Doubleday, 1970.

_____. *Poems 1957–1967*. Middletown, CT: Wesleyan University Press, 1967.

_____. *Self-Interviews*. Garden City, NY: Doubleday, 1970.

Djanikian, Gregory. *Falling Deeply into America*. Pittsburgh: Carnegie Mellon University Press, 1989.

Driscoll, Jack. *Fishing the Backwash*. Ithaca, NY: Ithaca House, 1984.

Dugan, Alan. *Poems*. New Haven: Yale University Press, 1961.

Dunn, Stephen. *New and Selected Poems 1974–1994*. New York: W. W. Norton, 1994.

Earle, Steve. "No. 29." *Exit 0* (CD). Uni/Mca, 1988.

Evans, David Allan. *Train Windows*. Athens: Ohio University Press, 1976.

_____. "Zen and the Art of Racquetball." *Aethlon* 12.1 (Fall 1994), 180.

Exley, Frederick. *A Fan's Notes*. New York: Random House, 1968.

Fairchild, B. H. *The Art of the Lathe*. Boston: Alice James Books, 1998.

Fitzgerald, Robert. *Spring Shade*. New York: New Directions, 1943.

Francis, Robert. *Collected Poems of Robert Francis*. Amherst: University of Massachusetts Press, 1959.

_____. *The Orb Weaver*. Middletown, CT: Wesleyan University Press, 1948.

Frost, Robert. *The Poetry of Robert Frost*. C. Latham, ed. New York: Holt, Rinehart and Winston, 1969.

Gallagher, Tess. *Amplitude: New and Selected Poems*. St. Paul, MN: Graywolf Press, 1978.

German, Norman. "New World in the Morning." *Worcester Review* 8.2 (Fall 1985), 68.

Ghigna, Charles. "A Fighter Learns of Hands." *Arete* 2.2 (Spring 1985), 168.

Gibb, Robert. *Momentary Days*. Camden, NJ: Walt Whitman Cultural Arts Center, 1989.

_____. "Night Basketball." *Arete* 3.2 (Spring 1986), 58.

Gilbert, Christopher. *Across the Mutual Landscape*. St. Paul, MN: Graywolf Press, 1984.

Gildner, Gary. *Blue Like the Heavens*. Pittsburgh: University of Pittsburgh Press, 1984.

_____. *The Warsaw Sparks*. Iowa City: University of Iowa Press, 1990.

Goldman, Judy. *Holding Back Winter*. Laurinburg, SC: St. Andrews University Press, 1987.

Greenway, William. "Spider Drill." *Arete* 3.2 (Spring 1986), 36.

Hamblin, Robert. "Half-Court Advantage." *Aethlon* 5.1 (Fall 1987), 179–180.

_____. "Pick and Roll." *Aethlon* 8.2 (Spring 1991), 14.

Harper, Michael S. *Images of Kin: New and Selected Poems*. Urbana: University of Illinois Press, 1977.

Heyen, William. *The Host: Selected Poems 1965–1990*. St. Louis: Time Being Books, 1994.

Bibliography of Primary Works

Hilberry, Conrad. *Sorting the Smoke: New and Selected Poems.* Iowa City: University of Iowa Press, 1990.

Hilton, David. *Huladance.* Trumansburg, NY: Crossing Press, 1976.

Hirsch, Edward. *The Night Parade.* New York: Alfred A. Knopf, 1989.

_____. *Wild Gratitude.* New York: Alfred A. Knopf, 1985.

Holden, Jonathan. *Design for a House: Poems.* Columbia: University of Missouri Press, 1972.

_____. *Falling from Stardom.* Pittsburgh: Carnegie Mellon University Press, 1984.

Homer. *The Iliad.* Richmond Lattimore, trans. Chicago: University of Chicago Press, 1974.

Horvath, Brooke. "Weathering March: Thoughts While Driving." *Arete* 2.2 (Spring 1985), 46.

Hudgins, Andrew. *Babylon in a Jar: New Poems.* Boston: Houghton Mifflin, 1998.

Huff, Michael. "A Radio Summer Evening in Nevada." *Southern Poetry Review* (Summer 1994), 29.

Hugo, Richard. "The Anxious Fields of Play." *The Real West Marginal Way.* New York: W. W. Norton, 1986, 31–50.

_____. *Making Certain It Goes On: The Collected Poems of Richard Hugo.* New York: W. W. Norton, 1984.

Humphries, Rolfe. *Collected Poems of Rolfe Humphries.* Bloomington: Indiana University Press, 1965.

Jackson, Richard. "Center Field." *Worlds Apart.* Tuscaloosa: University of Alabama Press, 1987.

Jarrell, Randall. *The Complete Poems.* New York: Farrar, Straus, and Giroux, 1969.

Jones, Rodney. *The Unborn.* Boston: Atlantic Monthly Press, 1985.

Kahn, Roger. *A Season in the Sun.* New York: Harper & Row, 1977.

Kinnell, Galway. *Mortal Acts, Mortal Words.* New York: Houghton Mifflin, 1980.

Komunyakaa, Yusef. *Magic City.* Middletown, CT: Wesleyan University Press, 1992.

Kumin, Maxine. *Connecting the Dots.* New York: W. W. Norton, 1996.

_____. *House, Bridge, Fountain, Gate.* San Francisco: Curtis Brown, 1975.

_____. *The Privilege.* New York: Harper & Row, 1965.

Lebow, Jeanne. "Running." *Arete* 1.2 (Spring 1984), 94.

Levine, Phillip. *What Work Is.* New York: Alfred A. Knopf, 1991.

Lieberman, Laurence. *The Unblinding.* New York: Macmillan, 1963.

Lindner, Carl. *Angling into Light.* Lewiston, NY: Mellen Poetry Press, 2001.

_____. *Shooting Baskets in a Dark Gymnasium.* N. Charleston, SC: Linwood Publishers, 1984.

Lipsitz, Lou. *Cold Water.* Middletown, CT: Wesleyan University Press, 1963.

Lynch, Janice. "Sixty-four Caprices for a Long-distance Swimmer: Notes on Swimming 100 Miles." *Beloit Poetry Journal* 37 (Fall 1986), 32–37.

McDonald, Cynthia. *(W)HOLES.* New York: Alfred A. Knopf, 1980.

McFee, Michael. *Vanishing Acts*. Frankfort, KY: Gnomon Press, 1989.

McKenna, J. J. Untitled poem. *Arete* 4.1 (1986): 170.

MacLeish, Archibald. *Collected Poems 1917–1952*. Boston: Houghton Mifflin, 1952.

Matthews, William. *Foreseeable Futures*. New York: Houghton Mifflin, 1992.

_____. *A Happy Childhood*. Boston: Little, Brown, 1984.

_____. *Selected Poems and Translations, 1969–1991*. NY: Houghton Mifflin, 1992.

_____. *Time and Money*. Boston: Houghton Mifflin, 1995.

Meinke, Peter. *Trying to Surprise God*. Pittsburgh: University of Pittsburgh Press, 1981.

Meschery, Tom. *Over the Rim*. New York: Popular Library, 1968.

Miller, Kevin. "Talking Back." *Aethlon* 11.2 (Spring 1994), 66.

Mitcham, Justin. *Somewhere in Ecclesiastes*. Springfield: University of Missouri Press, 1991.

Mizejewski, Linda. "Season Wish." *Hummers, Knucklers, and Slow Curves*, ed. Don Johnson, Urbana: University of Illinois, 1990.

Nyhart, Nina. "The Runner." *Poetry* (January 1998), 141.

Peeler, Tim. *Touching All the Bases*. Jefferson, NC: McFarland, 2000.

Piercy, Marge. *Circles on the Water*. New York: Alfred A. Knopf, 1982.

Pindar. *The Odes of Pindar*. Richmond Lattimore, trans. Chicago: University of Chicago Press, 1976.

Rainnie, Michael. "Line Coach." *Aethlon* 8.1 (1990), 191–92.

Ralph, Brett. "Practice Field." *Aethlon* 7.1 (1989), 129–30.

Ridl, Jack. *Between*. New Wilmington, PA: Dawn Valley Press, 1988.

Roberts, Kim. "The Players." *Aethlon* 6.2 (Spring 1989), 176.

Rubin, Larry. *Lanced in Light*. New York: Harcourt Brace Jovanovich, 1967.

Seibles, Tim. *Hurdy Gurdy*. Cleveland, OH: Cleveland State University Press, 1992.

Shannon, Mike. "The Art of Baseball Poetry." *Arete* 4.2 (Spring 1987), 146.

Sheehan, Tom. "Saturday Ceremonial." *Aethlon* 7.2 (1990), 41–42.

Shirley, Aleda. *Rilke's Children*. Monterey, KY: Larkspur Press, 1987.

Sklar, Danny. "Red Sox: 12 June, 1988." Unpublished poem.

Smith, Arthur. *Elegy on Independence Day*. Pittsburgh: University of Pittsburgh Press, 1985.

Smith, Barbara. "In Balance." *Aethlon* 5.1 (Fall 1987), 72.

Smith, Dave. *Cumberland Station*. Urbana: University of Illinois Press, 1977.

_____. *Fate's Kite*. Baton Rouge: Louisiana State University Press, 1995.

_____. *The Fisherman's Whore*. Athens: University of Ohio Press, 1974.

_____. *Goshawk, Antelope*. Urbana: University of Illinois Press, 1979.

_____. *In the House of the Judge*. New York: Harper and Row, 1983.

Smith, Ron. "Noseguard." *Arete* 3.1 (1985), 61–62.

_____. *Running Again in the Hollywood Cemetery*. Orlando: University of Central Florida Press, 1988.

Stafford, Darrell. "Travis Cox Dies on a Light Pole." *Kenyon Review* 9:2 (1989), 60.

Stone, Alison. "Nobody Left On." *Buffalo Spree* (Summer 1989), 107.

Bibliography of Primary Works

Stuart, Dabney. "Full Count." *Hummers, Knucklers, and Slow Curves*, ed. Don Johnson. Urbana: University of Illinois, 1990.

Swanson, Mark. "Where It Begins." *Aethlon* 5.2 (1988), 12.

Taylor, Marilyn. "Golden Warriors End Year with Big Loss." *Poetry* (July 1995), 222.

Torreson, Rodney. "Ten Years Retired, Bobby Murcer Makes a Comeback Bid, 1985." *Aethlon* 4.1 (Fall 1986), 180.

Troupe, Quincy. *Avalanche*. Minneapolis, MN: Coffee House Press, 1996.

_____. *Choruses*. Minneapolis, MN: Coffee House Press, 1999.

_____. *Skulls Along the River*. Berkeley, CA: Ishmael Reed Books, 1984.

Trudell, Dennis. *Fragments in Us: Recent and Earlier Poems*. Madison: University of Wisconsin Press, 1996.

_____. "The Years." *Aethlon* 11.2 (Spring 1994), 130.

Updike, John. *Collected Poems 1953–1993*. New York: Alfred A. Knopf, 1993.

Volkman, Karen. *Crash's Law*. New York: W. W. Norton, 1992.

Wakowski, Diane. *Emerald Ice: Selected Poems 1962–1987*. Black Sparrow Press, 1998.

Wallace, Robert. *Views from a Ferris Wheel*. New York: New Directions, 1965.

Wallace, Ronald. *The Uses of Adversity*. Pittsburgh: University of Pittsburgh Press, 1998.

Waterman, Cary. *When I Looked Back You Were Gone*. Minneapolis: Holy Cow Press, 1992.

Welch, Don. "To Bear Bryant, Somewhere on That Taller Tower." *Arete* 2.1 (Fall 1984).

Wheeler, Charles B. "Going to the Ballgame." *Aethlon* 7.2 (Spring 1990), 122–24.

White, Boyd. "Low Post." *Aethlon* 7.1 (Fall 1989), 121.

Whitman, Walt. *The Poetry and Prose of Walt Whitman*. Louis Untermeyer, ed. New York: Simon and Schuster, 1949.

Williams, William Carlos. *Selected Poems (1912–1962)*, Vol. I. New York: New Directions Publishing Corp., 1962.

Wormser, Baron. *When*. Louisville, KY: Sarabande Books, 1997.

Wright, James. *Collected Poems*. Middletown, CT: Wesleyan University Press, 1971.

Wright, Judith. *Collected Poems 1942–1970*. Sydney: Angus and Robertson, 1971.

Bibliography of Secondary Works

Bachelard, Gaston. *The Poetics of Reverie: Childhood, Language and the Cosmos.* Trans. Daniel Russell. Boston: Beacon Press, 1969.

Bandy, Susan J. "The Female Athlete as Protagonist: From Cynisca to Butcher." *Aethlon* 15.1 (Fall 1997), 83–97.

Bartky, Sandra. "Foucault, Femininity, and the Modernization of Patriarchal Power." In *Feminism and Foucault: Reflections on Resistance.* I. Diamond and L. Quimby, eds. Boston: Northeastern University Press, 1988, pp. 61–86.

Birrell, Susan, and Nancy Theberge. "Feminist Resistance and Transformation in Sport." In *Women and Sport: Interdisciplinary Perspectives.* D. Margaret Costa and Sharon R. Guthrie, eds. Champaign, IL: Human Kinetics, 1994, 361–376.

Bordo, Susan. *Unbearable Weight: Feminism, Western Culture, and the Body.* Berkeley: University of California Press, 1993.

Burns, Ken. "Watching Baseball on Green Fields of Memory." *New York Times,* 17 April 1992: B1.

Candelaria, Cordelia. *Seeking the Perfect Game: Baseball in American Literature.* Westport, CT: Greenwood Press, 1989.

Carson, Sharon, and Brooke Horvath. "Running in Place: The Lines and Miles of Grace Butcher's Life and Work." *Aethlon* 8.1 (1990): 119–30.

_____. "Women's Sports Poetry: Some Observations and Representative Texts." In *The Achievement of American Sport Literature: A Critical Appraisal.* Wiley Lee Umphlett, ed. Rutherford, Madison, and Teaneck, NJ: Fairleigh Dickinson University Press, 1991, 116–131.

Cixous, Helen. "The Laugh of the Medusa." In *Feminist Literary Theory: A Reader.* Mary Eagleton, ed. Oxford: Basil Blackwell, 1986, 225–227.

Dacey, Philip. "Challenging Chronos." *Aethlon* 6.1 (1987): 115–120.

Darden, Anne. "Outsiders: Women in Sport and Literature." *Aethlon* 15.1 (Fall 1997): 1–10.

Davis, Fred. *Yearning for Yesterday: A Sociology of Nostalgia.* New York: Free Press, 1979.

Bibliography of Secondary Works

Dickey, Christopher. *Summer of Deliverance*. New York: Touchstone Books, 1998.

Evans, David Allen. "Poetry and Sport." *Aethlon* 6.2 (1987): 141–45.

Giamatti, A. Bartlett. *Take Time for Paradise: Americans and Their Games*. New York: Summit Books, 1989.

Goldstein, Warren. "Inside Baseball." *Gettysburg Review* 3, 1992, 410–422.

Haas, Robert. "James Wright." In *The Pure Clear Word: Essays on the Poetry of James Wright*. Dave Smith, ed. Urbana: University of Illinois Press, 1982.

Hall, Donald. *Fathers Playing Catch with Sons: Essays on Sport*. San Francisco: North Point Press, 1985.

Hamblin, Robert. Unpublished paper, Popular Culture Association, 1991.

Harper, Ralph. *Nostalgia: An Existential Exploration of Longing and Fulfillment in the Modern Age*. Cleveland: Case Western Reserve Press, 1966.

Hassan, Ihab. *The Dismemberment of Orpheus: Toward a Post-Modern Literature*. New York: Oxford University Press, 1971.

Heaney, Seamus. *The Redress of Poetry*. New York: The Noonday Press, 1995.

"Heroes of the Spirit: An Interview with Dave Smith." *Graham House Review* (Spring 1982), 48–72.

Irigaray, Luce. *Ce Sexe qui n'en est pas un*. Paris: Editions de Minuit, 1977. Trans. in *New French Feminisms*: Amherst: University of Massachusetts Press, 1980.

Jones, Ann Rosalind. "'Writing the Body': Toward an Understanding of '*L'Écriture Feminine*.' In *The New Feminist Criticism*, ed. Elaine Showalter. New York: Pantheon, 1985, 361–377.

Kahn, Roger. *A Season in the Sun*. New York: Harper & Row, 1977.

Larner, Jeremy. *Drive, He Said*. New York: Dial, 1964.

Lever, Janet. *Soccer Madness*. Chicago: University of Chicago Press, 1983.

McDonnell, Thomas. "Bards at Bat." *Boston Globe Magazine*, 11 July 1982: 28–33.

May, Rollo. *Existence*. New York: Basic Books, 1958.

Messenger, Christian. *Sport and the Spirit of Play in Contemporary American Fiction*. New York: Columbia University Press, 1990.

Mitchie, Helena. *The Flesh Made Word: Female Figures and Women's Bodies*. New York: Oxford University Press, 1987.

Nelson, Mariah Burton. *Are We Winning Yet? How Women Are Changing Sports and Sports Are Changing Women*. New York: Random House, 1991.

_____. *The Stronger Women Get, the More Men Love Football: Sexism and the American Culture of Sports*. New York: Harcourt Brace, 1994.

The Norton Book of Sports. Plimpton, George, ed. New York: W. W. Norton, 1992.

Novak, Michael. *The Joy of Sports*. New York: Basic Books, 1976.

Oglesby, Carol. Epilogue. In *Sport, Men and the Gender Order: Critical Feminist Perspectives*. M. A. Messner and D. F. Sabo, eds. Champaign, IL: Human Kinetics, 1990, 241–245.

Oriard, Michael. "From Jane Allen to Water Dancer: A Brief History of the Feminist (?) Sports Novel." *Modern Fiction Studies* 33 (1987): 9–20.

_____. "Professional Football as Cultural Myth." *Journal of American Culture* 4.3 (1981): 27–41.

Ostriker, Alicia. "In Mind: The Divided Self in Women's Poetry." In *Poetics: Essays on the Art of Poetry*. George Murphy and Paul Mariani, eds. Green Harbor, MA: Tendril Press, 1986, 111–138.

Porter, Denis. "The Perilous Quest: Baseball as Folk Drama." *Critical Inquiry* 4.1 (1977), 143–58.

Roberts, Terrence, J. "The Making and Remaking of Sports Actions." *Journal of the Philosophy of Sport* XIII (1986), 89–94.

_____. "Sport and Strong Poetry." *Journal of the Philosophy of Sport* 22 (1995), 94–107.

Rorty, Richard. *Contingency, Irony and Solidarity*. Cambridge, MA: Cambridge University Press, 1989.

Rosenthal, M. L. *Poetry and the Common Life*. Oxford: Oxford University Press, 1974.

Ross, Murray. "Football Red and Baseball Green." In *Sport Inside Out*. David L. Vanderwerken and Spencer K. Wertz, eds. Ft. Worth: Texas Christian University Press, 1985.

Smith, Dave. *Local Assays on Contemporary American Poetry*. Urbana: University of Illinois Press, 1985.

Sports Fans: The Psychology and Social Impact of Spectators. Daniel J. Wann, Merrill J. Melnick, Gordon G. Russell, and Russell Pease, eds. Champaign, IL: Human Kinetics, 1991.

Stefanile, Felix. "Poetry That Reaches Out." *The Christian Science Monitor*, January 17, 1992, 14.

Vanderwerken, David. "James Dickey's Elegy for Lombardi." *Arete* 3.1 (Fall 1985): 137–142.

Vendler, Helen. *Seamus Heaney*. Cambridge, MA: Harvard University Press, 1998.

Weinstein, Arnold. "A Romance with the Classics." *Lincoln Arts Center Review* 28 (Spring 2001), 9.

Woodard, Charles, and David Allan Evans, eds. *The Sport of Poetry, the Poetry of Sport*. Brookings, SD: No publisher listed, 1983.

Index

Index

Index

Index